How Could I Not Believe?

The Spiritual Journey of a True American Family

by

Gloria Sorrentino Vanacore

ISBN: 0692347518
ISBN-13: 9780692347515

DEDICATION

To My Family

Cover by
Carol S. Johnson

Table Of Contents

I am a little pencil in the hand of a writing God

who is sending a love letter to the world.

www.catholic bible101.com

ACKNOWLEDGMENTS

To all the members of the Legion of Mary who have inspired me and to those who are still in service, especially Laura and Marlene, my close friends and partner sisters in service. My gratitude is also extended to Gayle Smith who spent many very special moments with me, lovingly transcribing my tattered and faded notes gathered throughout the years of my life for this book. I would also like to acknowledge my sister, Frances Vassallo, and my nieces Candy Sorrentino McMahon and Emily Sorrentino Sloane. By the way, thank you, Dolly Tucker, for planning my 90th birthday celebration and family reunion—the best birthday party–a party we will never forget. Many thanks from the family. Finally, a sincere thank you and deep appreciation is extended to Jean Brogan, my closest neighbor and friend, and to all of my other beautiful friends here in Las Vegas, Nevada.

Gloria (bottom left) with her sister, Frances, and brother, Ciro, (bottom center and right), and parents, Emilia and Amedeo Sorrentino (above)

Foreword

Gloria Sorrentino Vanacore was born in Brooklyn, New York, in 1924. She was the second child of Emilia and Amedeo Sorrentino, preceded by an older brother, Ciro (Duke), and followed by a younger sister, Frances. In 1929 she attended Sacred Heart Catholic School in Brooklyn and was taught by the Missionary Sisters of the Sacred Heart. The school was founded by Mother Cabrini who was later canonized as St. Frances Xavier Cabrini. She went on to attend the Girls' Commercial High School in Brooklyn where she graduated in June of 1942. Immediately following graduation, she worked in New York City for Gibbs & Cox, a firm of shipbuilders and designers for the U.S. Navy during World War II, and also worked a second job at Gimbel's Department Store in the evenings. In 1944 Gloria and her family moved to Colonial Road in Brooklyn across the street from a cloistered monastery.

On September 28, 1947, Gloria Sorrentino became Mrs. Victor Anthony Vanacore. They were married at St. Patrick's Catholic Church on Fort Hamilton Parkway in Brooklyn. Her husband was born in New Haven, Connecticut, in 1918. For the first ten years of their marriage, they rented the first floor of Victor's parents' home for $35.00 a month at 132 Oakley Street in New Haven, Connecticut. In 1956 Mr. Vanacore traded a boat for an unfinished lot on Blakeslee Avenue in North Haven, Connecticut. The Vanacores built their family home there and moved into it a year later. They had six children who were born in the following order: Victor Anthony, 1948; Paul Joseph, 1950; Madelyn Mary, 1951; Robert Allan, 1953; Arthur Michael (Chuck), 1955; and David John, 1962. In the back of their new home, much to the enjoyment of the children, there was a good-sized pond where they went swimming, fishing, water skiing, ice skating, and played ice hockey.

Today, Gloria Vanacore continues her devotion to both her Eucharistic Ministry and to El Jen Convalescent Home, reciting the Rosary and visiting the sick. Gloria is presently a member of the St. Elizabeth Ann Seaton Parish in Summerlin and of the Parish Adoration Society.

With five sons and daughters-in-law, one daughter and a son-in-law, 15 grandchildren, and 9 great-grandchildren, she keeps very busy with her large family. The original Vanacore Connecticut family is now spread across six states: California, Nevada, New York, West Virginia, New Jersey, and Florida. Gloria spends part of each summer in Southern California, and those who meet her feel touched instantly by her spirituality, vitality, love of life, and faith. My admiration and love for her has grown as I've gotten to know her and her life story. This amazing 89 year-old truly has a zest for life, a benevolent heart, and a concern for the well-being of all people. I feel so fortunate to know her.

Written by Gloria's friend, Cellist: Gayle Smith

Chapter One

In My Own Words

This book is about how I grew up, got married, raised our six children, and found my strongest spiritual faith in, of all places—Las Vegas: a place they call "Sin City"! It is a book of facts, true life experiences, and especially about my trust and faith in God. My beliefs are what prompted me to write this book. I sincerely hope for all of you who read this book a life of love void of complicated issues and unnecessary worries. Nine times out of ten, we will later realize that many of our worries and issues are brought upon us by ourselves. This book is not being written with the intention of getting a Pulitzer Prize or to be a best seller. If it reaches the hearts of my family, readers, and my many friends, I will be gratified.

Some of you who begin to read this book and who do not believe there is a God will find my story very difficult to understand. After I began to write, I was told I had to write about myself—that in order for me to let you understand the real meaning of my book, you would have to understand *me*. "No," I thought. "This is not about me! Lord, how could I ask my readers to believe that all things are possible with You and impossible without You, since they really neither know *me* nor what makes me feel the way I do?" I asked myself, "Do I begin *when* my life began? Or where my life began? *Or* when I came to the realization that life can be beautiful?"

There really isn't much to tell about myself. There were times I felt that I lived a very mundane existence. I was a city girl born and raised in Brooklyn, New York. I attended Catholic School from 1929 to 1938, and it was not an easy road for me. In my class book our Mother Superior wrote, "Perseverance and prayers will lead you on your road to success." God! I couldn't do a thing without asking the Lord for help. I do believe that many of my principles and ideas about life were instilled in me when I went to Sacred Heart School.

Although I've attempted to sit down and write my story many times, I have often found myself saying, "Just one more year—or maybe next year." The years have been fleeting by, and now it is time to offer my book to readers. I aspire to reach people of all ages and denominations: the rich and the poor, prisoners, the handicapped, the homeless, lost souls, people of this new generation, anyone and someone in any other situation. I believe what happened to me could happen to you or to anyone who believes in himself or herself and in God. All good things can happen to those who let themselves be open and receptive to the great blessings of our Lord. If they do this, their lives can be beautiful. The love and mercy of God is here for all who believe or wish to believe that they too can have a good, a healthy, and a happy life.

As I am in the process of recounting the course of uplifting events or "happenings" in my life, it seems like they all occurred close to each other. Yet, in reality they happened far apart, sometimes even by years. I call these events "blessings." Most of my blessings came in the latter part of my life. At least I thought they did, since I was never aware before that some of these gifts had most likely been with me all the time. How foolish I was not to realize and appreciate those blessed moments earlier in my life. As time went by, I found myself wanting to share my story with others but never felt it would be possible. Now, with the help of modern technology, here I am! Any senior who has reached my age has a story to tell, so why am I writing mine? I am hoping and praying that with the help of My Lord and Our Blessed Mother, I can make a difference in the lives of others.

Me? Who am I? I am a person of God. I am YOU! At this point in my life, there is something deep inside of me, telling me that I must shout out to all of you who are willing to read, listen, and feel with an open mind and open heart. Therefore, I am not writing this book for myself, but for you who are willing to *believe* in yourselves and in the *Love of God* before you leave this life. Before I begin to reveal my beautiful and heartfelt blessings and sometimes painful experiences, I must say that in the back of my mind, I always have had a sense of peace and love in my heart for God. I believe this was what kept me going through all the years of children and relatives in and out of our house, even though I never consciously thought about it.

Living here in Las Vegas has been a unique experience. Most of my family and friends first thought, and some may still think, "Oh, there's Gloria, she always loved the glitz and the gambling!" But I would respond, "No! How wrong they really are." I have found a peace here in Las Vegas, believe it or not, that I did not find in any of the other places that I have lived: Brooklyn, New York, New Haven and North Haven, Connecticut, and Southern California. There always had been a feeling of emptiness inside of me until in Las Vegas I started to realize what life is really all about! At that time I felt in my heart that my husband and I had brought up six beautiful children—but now what? My life still seemed so empty. What is life? Fun and games? What is success? Money? Power? I had a great need for fulfillment, but not the need to impress anyone. All that I wanted was to feel good about myself.

While attending Mass one Sunday at St. Francis de Sales Church in Las Vegas, I heard our pastor, Monsignor La Voy, mention the *Legion of Mary*, a Catholic laity service group. I immediately felt a desire to join, since I knew I *had* to do something to enrich my life. My new journey of life was about to begin, and you will understand how this happened as my story unfolds. Now where am I going with this? As I close this chapter, I flash to thoughts of my children who always loved and respected me.

Let's start with my first born, Victor. He was named after his dad. He was a handful from the beginning, quite a feisty, energetic child who was always getting into trouble. He and my youngest son, David, both later went into the music profession. While I was at home taking care of the other children, the Sisters of Mercy at St. Michael's School offered to look after Victor in their nursery during the day. At the time I thought, Lord, have mercy on the poor nuns! Our second son, Paul, came soon after Victor. He was completely the opposite, much more docile. Thanks be to God, he was calm, quiet, and loving—much easier to handle! A year later, with diligent prayers and hope, came my dear little girl, Madelyn, named after her dad's mother. I loved the name Mary, and fortunately for her or should I say for me, we named her *Madelyn Mary*. She was born in May, one of my favorite months.

In my early years of married life, my children sure kept me busy, but with the Lord's help I was able to manage all the turmoil. Two years later another wonderful son, Robert, came along who now likes to call himself the one in the middle, and two years after that Arthur (Chuck), another blessed son. Chuck would follow closely in his father's footsteps. After seven more years my baby, David, was born. He was quite a nice surprise! Yes, things were hectic but strangely enough I never did give it a thought. My prayers were always there, asking God to watch over the children and their dad. I thank My Lord for giving me a healthy "crop." It was not easy and it seemed like a life I never expected. I am sure there are many of us who have felt that way at some time or another in our lives. There were times when I said to myself, "Lord, this is not me! Not *my* life! Not what I wanted nor intended!"

Our life was not easy financially. My husband, Vic, was a mechanic. He loved his children and tried to do the best he could. As a father he was a good disciplinarian and a church-going man. He made sure that all the children went with him to 9:00 a.m. Mass on Sunday mornings. I would always try to make the earlier Mass and then go back home to get the children ready for their Mass. Of course this went on for years. They can all attest to the fact that although life wasn't a bed of roses, it was still a good and healthy life. As for me, with my trust in my God, I tried to do the best I could—and I readily admit that I could not have done it without my daily prayers.

Again Jesus spoke to them, saying, "I am the light of the world. Whoever follows me will not walk in darkness but will have the light of life."

John 8:12

Chapter Two
The Early Years

I was born Gloria Claire Sorrentino on November 5, 1924, to my parents, Amedeo and Emilia (Emily) Sorrentino in Brooklyn, New York. My father was born in Sorrento, Italy, in 1890 and immigrated to America in 1907. He was a U.S. Army veteran of World War I (1914-1918). My mother, Emily, was born in Brooklyn in 1896, the daughter of Italian immigrants from Naples. My mom and dad were great parents, and I loved them dearly. They made a beautiful couple. My dad loved my mother very much. It seemed to me that she came first, and I did not mind, because she came first in my life too. But loving her did not make him a softer person. He was to be obeyed and heard. He would say, "I make the rules! No bending!"

He was not a believer in the Catholic faith, but I know that he believed in God. Every Christmas he would put the Nativity Scene under our tree. We would light candles and sing our Italian Christmas hymn, "Tu Scendi Dalle Stelle." He seldom attended Mass, only if I begged him, and I never saw him with Rosary Beads or the Bible. I didn't mind, as long as he loved my Baby Jesus. I realized that religious faith was something I could not force on my dad, but I knew he had faith *inside* himself. He was a good man. Mom was different; she went to Mass every Sunday and had a little altar in her room.

My mom was not a frail woman. As a matter of fact, she was quite robust and stood 5'7" tall. I certainly did not ever measure up at 5' 1" to her stature—one of my main complaints! People would tell me that we resembled one another. I could never see it. She seemed so beautiful and had such a striking personality. She was sweet and loving, always pleasant with people, and she had many friends. I still remember Mom making her Duncan Hines pound cakes. She would take them over to her friends who she always visited when they became ill. They called her "Aunt Em" - a name the neighborhood never forgot.

I always felt that I could never measure up to Mom. I loved her so much, as she did me. I always also felt that she favored my younger sister and older brother. Yet I knew in my heart that when she looked at me, I felt the loving nature of her smile. She may have wished that I could be more like my sister, especially as we were growing up, but I knew she loved me. My sister, Fran, had a beauty about her. She was much taller and she was a blonde. It was the "in thing" to be blonde ("blondes have more fun!"), and being the baby my mom adored her. Actually Fran was like Mom in a way. She loved clothes and jewelry. I was not a "fashionista" but more of a "Plain Jane". I never attached importance to those things.

While growing up, my mother would have my clothes made by one of my cousins. I was chubby at the time, and clothes for me were hard to come by. Mom used to tell me that I needed more makeup and would want me to visit her beauty shop more often. I did like to look nice but held back. I think it was because my best neighborhood friend, Lucy Licata (Lulu), had lost her own mom at age ten. She was one of nine children. She came from a less fortunate family, and I was especially careful not to "out-dress" her as we were growing up. When people saw Lulu and me together, they called us "Me and my Shadow" or "Two-in-One Shoe Polish," because we seemed inseparable. Dear Lulu died years later in 2009. Though we lived many miles apart during our adult years, our hearts always had a great connection. I don't believe anyone ever knew me as well as Lulu did.

As a child it was great fun bicycling, roller skating, and playing games like hopscotch, jacks, marbles, checkers, and Simon Says. Although we never dressed up on Halloween, it was our tradition to dress up on Thanksgiving Day. It seems ironic to me now that I chose to dress up as a nun. I also made Novenas for Special Intentions (i.e. requests). My father had grapevines in the backyard and in autumn would make his own wine in the basement. In those days milk was only available in glass gallons. We had large ice blocks delivered to the house, and my father who liked seltzer also had cases of it delivered. To wash the clothes, my mother used a washboard and hung the laundry on the suspended rotating clotheslines out back with wooden clothes pins. When it was cold, the sheets would freeze!

Having an older brother and a younger sister who seemed to get most of the attention, I always felt left out. I don't believe that my parents caused this feeling intentionally, but they must have felt inside that I was the strongest one of the three children. I can see this and understand it now because as we grew up, I was always there for everyone's ups and downs. They would all actually ask me for advice. Even then, I never thought of my advice being connected to my faith in My God. Nevertheless, I kept trying to help if I could, praying and hoping Dad would go to Sunday Mass with me. He would go now and then just to please me, although I knew he didn't really have his heart in it. I would still have sleepless nights from a fear that he would go to Hell (as the nuns told me in Catechism class).

Life at Sacred Heart School

A Wing and a Prayer!

I attended Sacred Heart Catholic School in Brooklyn from 1929 to 1938. Sacred Heart was founded by St. Francis Cabrini and run by the Missionary Sisters of Sacred Heart and the Mother Cabrini Nuns. We wore black uniforms with light brown collars and cuffs and a school emblem embroidered on the uniform in gold. Our home was quite a distance from the school, so one of my cousins, Jack, would walk several of us in our neighborhood to school. I recall the cold, bitter, snowy days in winter. There were times when our fingers and feet would get numb.

I still remember well what the nuns taught me in school. They were devoted to providing us with an excellent education and also to teaching us about God. Three questions were embedded in my mind:

1. *Who made you?* God made me.
2. *Why did God make you?* God made me to love, honor, and serve Him.
3. *Where is God?* God is everywhere!

As a child in school, and even later in life, who could ever forget those fundamental questions posed to me by the nuns faithfully from day one? However, truthfully speaking, I couldn't get away fast enough from Catholic School with all of their strict rules and regulations! Even so I still felt a sense of security, seeing the statue of Mother Cabrini daily in the corner of the classroom.

Growing up as a child, I don't remember having many friends, but I do remember those few that I did have. There was my closest friend, Lulu; Carmella Esposito, my best friend at Sacred Heart; and my friend and neighbor, Cosmo Saporito (nicknamed Gus) who later went on to become a priest and Monsignor. Gus was brilliant and helped me, day after day, with my homework. I was not the brightest student, but with diligent prayer and hard work, I managed to become a B student. Trust me, being a B student was great for being in a Catholic school and having the nuns at your back all the time. They were by no means gentle. They were stern and would teach with pointer in hand and—I might add—with no mercy!

If homework was not done, "Do not come to class." If late, "Go to the end of the line." In quiz exams it was like a competition almost every day. We all tried so hard to work ourselves to be up in the top seven. Me compete? I tried so much just to get to the top seven. I ended up there by the skin of my teeth. And again, with diligent prayers and my trust in God, you can't imagine how hard I had prayed to reach my goal. Back then I don't believe anything came easily. I always needed "a wing and a prayer."

It was while I was attending Sacred Heart that I joined the *Children of Mary*, a society at the school. Deep in my heart I still never felt that I had anything special inside of me. I just went on with my life. I do remember being devoted and always received the Holy Eucharistic (Communion) on the First Friday of every month. I am mentioning this because I feel that perhaps this is where my deep devotion to God and to Our Blessed Mother began.

Reverend Monsignor
Cosmo G. Saporito

1924 - 2011

He planted trees
under whose shade
He might never sit.

My First Vision

My spiritual journey began in 1931 when I received my First Communion. Soon after that, my mother's aunt Annie passed away, and the family discussed at length where the casket was to be placed in the house. At that time many of the deaths in the parish had "viewings": when the body of the deceased would lie in state in the home. Much to my surprise—and fear, they decided to place my dear aunt's body in the room right next to mine. That night I cried myself into a deep sleep, and that is when I had my first vision of the Blessed Mother.

I saw her as clear as day under a doorway in my bedroom. She looked at me with a smile, nodded her head. and said to me, *Do not fear, I will always be near.* I can still see her as clear as day! From that day on I felt a sort of serenity and a strong faith, which at times I find so hard to explain; but I believe God can, in time.

How Could I Not Believe?

When I think about it, I still can't believe what is happening to our beautiful world that God created. Was it created for this? Created for a world of destruction? It is still frightening to me. Does thinking about it do the same thing to you?

Gloria Vanacore

Chapter Three

Then and Now

Thank God, graduation day from Sacred Heart arrived. I went on to attend Girls' Commercial High School, now Prospect High School, in Brooklyn. I enjoyed going to high school and found it so much easier, since I did not feel under as much pressure. By then I felt I was studying at my own pace. I cannot complain about my high school years. As a matter of fact, they were fun and I enjoyed my friends and classes.

In high school we wore long torso dresses. The hem length was mid-calf. I pushed my mound of curly hair back on my head with a ribbon that would match my dress. That's as far as the "fashionista" in me went! Through all of this, I just kept dreaming and hoping that someday I would finally graduate. Then I would be able to work and earn a good paycheck so we could move out of our old neighborhood. I never did like the one I was raised in. As I recall, it was close to the "Red Hook" section of Brooklyn.

I remember one strange encounter when I was about 16. My dearest friend, Lulu, and I were visiting another friend in the neighborhood. That evening was a strange one. Most of the conversation revolved around ghosts and the paranormal. One of the girls brought in a Ouija board. Not knowing what it was about at that time, we played it as if it was a fun game. When I look back now, it should have scared me out of my wits! Why did I do that?

As I write, I find myself going back in time and asking, what and who caused me to do things? And what caused me to think and feel the way I did? In high school the future "Father Gus" was *still* meeting me at the bus stop. He was concerned about how I was doing in my classes. I always admired his intelligence and wished I could have had even one ounce of his brains. Whoever would have thought that *he* would become a Monsignor? He must have loved his studies in Seminary. As for me, the only courses I really enjoyed in *my* schooling were my accounting and swimming classes. But there was always some sort of a connection between us.

When they say "then and now," how quickly times have changed now! They are changing every moment of every day. There is no end, and I don't believe there will ever be an end in technology changing our basic values and ideas. But the only thing that will never change for certain, as I write my story, is "In God We Trust." Today we take so much for granted, and we take life so lightly—and never stop to consider what life is really all about.

A Dream Come True

Gus and I both graduated high school in 1942. When I graduated from Girls' Commercial High School, I knew that my mother was proud of me. I believe it was because neither she nor my dad remembered that, as a sophomore, I had asked them if I could drop out! My request made them furious. Mom said, "Gloria, *please* let us be proud of you!" Well, I thank God that I did graduate! Of course I'd do anything to please them. It made me feel so good about myself. I thought maybe someday I could enter into a college. But that didn't happen. Gus went into the Navy and I went out to work. Believe it or not, I was employed two weeks after graduation with a job at Gibbs & Cox that I would enjoy for five years. I wanted to keep working and have an income of my own.

My First Employment
"A Cross in My Pocket"

My first job interview was at Gibbs & Cox, a firm that designed ships for the U.S. Navy. There were four of us, all girls, applying for the position. I truly might add they were *all* better students than I could ever be. I was a little nervous at first, but I had a cross in my pocket. I don't even remember saying a prayer, although I may have been thinking of it at the time. I beckoned to my friends to go into the admittance room first. I wasn't frightened, but I always wanted to be the last one. For some crazy reason, as they came out from their interviews, they were all told the same thing—that their applications would be "kept on file." I was shocked! Right after my interview, they hired me that very day!

I said to myself, "I can't believe it … them hiring me?" The girls before me were much more intelligent and had so much more to offer, but the company chose me. Was it luck? I don't think so. It had to be the hand of God. I ran home and told my parents. They were as happy as I was and I began working the following week. It was a great experience to work with such wonderful people. It was so exciting. I couldn't believe I could do it. I enjoyed going to work and being among the nice people I worked with, who also became my good friends. I felt so good about myself and, yes, it was always God's hand on my shoulder all of the time but little did I realize it at the time! This was the only full-time job I held until the week I got married.

At the time, I believed that my job would be the beginning of a new life for me. I could work and help my mom and dad get a new home somewhere on Shore Road, my favorite neighborhood in Brooklyn. It wasn't yet the end of my first year of employment, when I would plead with my dad to move there; I begged him to take the step and move there. I promised him, "I will help you with every paycheck I make!" Gosh—I felt so good. I knew it was going to happen! We ended up buying a duplex across from a cloistered monastery. Every now and then, I would stop in at their garden to say a prayer. For me it was a "dream come true." I worked hard, and I might add that dreams do come true when you believe in yourself.

From typing in a secretarial pool, I worked my way up to become a personal secretary for Mr. Garner who was one of the firm's top architects, and I believed he was the sweetest and most gentle person on this earth. Secretly during the day, I would thank God for being there. I worked very hard to make money to help my parents purchase the house. I used to hand my paycheck to my father without opening it, as I was the one who had convinced my parents to move. It was a big move for them and I felt responsible. I had always wanted the "American Dream" for our family, and Colonial Road was one of the most prestigious neighborhoods in Brooklyn. I worked extra hours on weekends and was paid double time. The house was worth every penny—the great American Dream had finally come true for us.

There was a little time for fun too, and in those days dancing was my passion. Lulu and I would meet and catch the subway or bus to one of the dance halls or nightclubs featuring live bands. We danced to the bands of the Dorsey Brothers, Glenn Miller, Xavier Cougat with Carmen Miranda singing, Vaughan Monroe, Louis Prima, Gene Krupa, and Buddy Rich. Those were the days of the dance marathons. We enjoyed dancing the Tango, Rhumba, Samba, Mambo, Cha Cha, Peabody, Fox Trot, and Waltz. I loved dancing and even won several dance contests.

During the summers my friends and I would go on vacation to Atlantic City and Luna Park on the Jersey Shore. We also enjoyed listening to stories on the radio and to Frank Sinatra, Tony Bennett, Perry Como, and Dean Martin. When we went to the movies, most of them were cowboy movies, starring actors such as William Boyd, Tom Mix, Gene Autry, Roy Rogers, and Dale Evans.

On Sunday, December 7, 1941, a bombshell hit us! On that day, as I recall, my girlfriend Lulu and I were walking along Court Street in Brooklyn, New York to the movie theatre. Suddenly, we heard the loud, clamouring voices of the newsboys in the streets. Since we had no television the newspaper boys were yelling, "EXTRA! EXTRA! The Japanese have just bombed Pearl Harbor!" Lulu and I looked at each other! We were stunned! People around us looked as if they were in a trance, "Not our beautiful country: our 'Land of the Free'! Being invaded?" We were tempted to go back home because we were both *so* frightened. Then, I remember so clearly President Roosevelt's announcement to the nation on the radio. He called it "A Day of Infamy" and brought the United States into World War II. Our government began rationing just about everything: food, oil, coffee ... they even limited gasoline. The slogan "Use it up, wear it out, make it do—or do without it!" echoed everywhere on the home front

We lost about 3,000 people at Pearl Harbor on that infamous day, just about as many as we would also lose years later on September 11, 2001—another day we will never forget. That was the morning of the terrorist attack on the World Trade Center in New York, another catastrophic event! Although it happened 68 years later that day, too, scared the living daylights out of me! I got on my knees and prayed, "Lord, not again!"

On both of those tragic days crisis brought us all together. Now with all that is happening today, our country often seems to be even more divided now than it was then. Again, I wonder *when* this state of affairs will end. Or—will it ever? When I think about it, I still can't believe what is happening to our beautiful world that God created.

Was it created for this? Created for a world of destruction? It is still frightening to me. Does thinking about all of this do the same thing to you?

Believe in yourselves and in the Love of God
before you leave this life.

... Gloria Vanacore

Gloria Sorrentino (right) with her future husband, Victor Vanacore (center), and her best friend, Lucille "Lulu" Licata (left). Lulu is wearing her bridesmaid's dress. She had been in a wedding earlier that day.

Chapter Four

What God Hath Joined Together . . .

On September 28, 1947, I married Victor Anthony Vanacore at St. Patrick's Catholic Church on Fort Hamilton Parkway in Brooklyn. I soon would feel my nightmare begin. At least it seemed like one. Why? It's a question most of us would ask ourselves. I did not know what was to happen in my future. Do any of us really know? Do you? Marriage is such an important step. I didn't take it lightly before I married Victor. In fact, I was really terrified. First of all, my husband-to-be was a good friend of the family. He was born and raised in New Haven and of Italian descent like I was. His mom and dad were both Italian immigrants, and he had three brothers and one sister. His eldest brother John had married my first cousin, Olympia.

I had met Victor once when I was 16 years old on a beach at a family gathering in Point Pleasant, New Jersey. At first I thought, "Gosh, he's cute." I liked him, but he seemed so much more mature. It seemed, at the time, he was attracted to me, but I never gave it a second thought. I didn't see him again until I was 21 years old. So I only knew him vaguely from the meeting five years earlier. My mom invited him to my 21st birthday party, the first party I remember ever having in my life. I don't think my mom believed in birthday parties. I guess she thought I wouldn't mind if she invited a few of my favorite friends. A few weeks later, Victor called and asked if I'd like to go out with him. I was 21 years old and he was 27. I was excited, but I never dreamed that on our first date–*Yes, first date*—that he would ask me to marry him!

I remember his proposal. He said, "Do you think you could put up with me the rest of your life?" I replied, "Are you nuts? I hardly know you." When I came home that evening, Mom was at the door anxiously waiting for me. She wanted to know about our date and if I'd had a good time. I said, "Mom, I don't believe it. He asked me if I *would marry him!* I hardly know him!" Of course I did not know what he was really like. She looked at me with that beautiful loving smile and said, "Oh, Gloria, you would make me the happiest mother in the world. He is a good boy, and I know his family." This really got to me. I loved my mother so much. My dad chimed in, "He will be a good provider and a hard worker." I was still hesitant, not knowing Victor that well. I was still trying to figure out who and what I wanted in *my* life. A husband and family? Or a career? Loving my beautiful mom, dad, and family, I thought, "God, what must I do?"

We married and that was the year that my life went into complete turmoil. Truthfully I thought, "What a disaster!" I never felt that it was a decision my family made *for* me, because it was really my decision. My mom had never said, "You *must* marry him." Rather she would say things like, "We've known the family *so long* ..." Now what did I actually think of Victor? Yes, at the time he was handsome, sincere, and caring. We had dated for a year and a half, during which time I only saw him a couple of times a month. I never dreamed or felt that it was such a crucial decision. However, from our wedding day forward there were disappointments, troublesome years, and desperate hours, along with many strange experiences taking place.

Although it was not really an arranged marriage, it sure seemed that way. I realize and believe now that it was a scenario and test that the Lord was putting me through. I kept thinking, "Did I make the right choice? What am I doing? Moving out of my beautiful home that my mom and dad provided for me—and that we *all* worked so hard to get?" I still think of those many years that I had with my wonderful family—the people I loved so much. It was a *home* I had really looked forward to living in. I *still* loved living there with my family. I assure you—my prayers were working overtime the day I got married.

We chose to go to Washington, D.C. on our honeymoon. That was the first disaster! I sat beside Victor in the car and felt I looked rather chic in my going away outfit—a blue suit with a matching pillbox hat. Apparently he already did not know or respect me well enough. He looked over at me and said, "I don't like that hat." At that moment we were crossing the Brooklyn Bridge. He opened the window, pulled the hat off of my head and threw it over the railing into the Hudson River! I thought, "Is he *nuts* or what?" Gosh, I felt like hitting him over the head with my purse and throwing *him* into the river! Maybe he thought he had a sense of humor, but I was enraged and failed to see any humor. I thought to myself, "Who or what did I marry?" Was I thinking straight when I said, "Yes" to him? I don't think so. In the back of my mind I knew I was making my mother happy, and I guess that was all that mattered to me. At first I questioned my dad and told him, "Gosh, Papa, I never thought he'd be like that."

I decided to put that "hat scene" under the rug, but I never forgot it. As we go on, you will see that it is so easy to hurt someone. To forgive is more difficult. Looking back I believe that Mom had an agenda. She probably said to herself, "This is a good time to get my daughter to meet someone we love and trust. Victor Vanacore is a fine man from a good family." So did the match work? For Mom and the family? Yes. As for me, I continued to have my doubts. Again my prayers were working overtime. Sometimes I would look at Vic and want to throw my shoe at him. (That would become a favorite tale of mine as we brought up our six children.)

So the honeymoon was over very soon, and it seemed my marriage was falling apart before it had begun. I started feeling such an emptiness inside me—like one I'd never felt before.

Our First Home

We moved into a three-story home on Oakley Street in New Haven, Connecticut. We rented the first floor apartment from Victor's mother for $35 a month. His father and mother, Noni Madeline, lived on the top floor. My cousin, Olympia, who married John (Vic's brother), lived on the second floor, and Vic and I had the first floor. One big happy family (*ahem!*). I felt very isolated there. In the back of my mind I was always thinking, "What am I doing here, of all places on this earth?" I would think of my life before my marriage, living in Brooklyn with subways, trolley cars, and buses for transportation, and the best parents a person could ask for. That was all that I had known. Now I felt like I had been pushed onto "this Godforsaken farm-like way of life"! In the beginning it hadn't been half as bad, since Vic drove me into Brooklyn to visit my family every other week, as he promised he would—until I got pregnant.

Thank God, I did get pregnant soon, because I did not like living in that town and I still felt, somehow, as if I'd made a grave mistake. I was not happy and there were family difficulties. I was lonely inside. I needed to fill the void I had, and I couldn't wait for my life to have meaning. At the time I despised the house on Oakley Street, but later realized I really should have loved it. It was there, where My Lord gave me my first child – the first in our family of six children who are all so devoted and caring today.

God's Very Special Gifts

On June 28, 1948, I was blessed with my first-born son, Victor Anthony. Victor couldn't have been born any sooner. It was a joy. However, as the family walked in and out of my first floor apartment, I felt I never had any privacy. It was not really *my* space. Needless to say, my weekend visits to see my mother and father went from between weeks to months. Eighteen months later my second son, Paul Joseph, came along in 1950, then my daughter Madelyn Mary in 1951 whom the family loved dearly. When my niece, Claire, found out I was pregnant a few months after Paul was born, she had mentioned how nice it would be to have a girl. We went together and prayed for a girl in front of the Blessed Mother statue, all nine months of my pregnancy! And as the Lord blessed us Madelyn Mary was born on May 21st—on Claire's birthday! How impressive that must have been in Claire's heart and mind. After that, she became devoted to the Blessed Mother.

As the Lord would have it, Madelyn Mary was the sweetest young lady and a great help to me as the other children were growing up. She was such a joy to have around and was a profound influence in the lives of her brothers. As she grew up Madelyn always held a desire to leave Connecticut. In 1974 she decided to move to Southern California, where she moved into a condominium in Santa Monica with her cousin, Claire.

How Could I Not Believe?

The children's toddler years were great. They all played together and got into trouble together. There was not a day that went by that I did not ask my Lord for help. I did everything alone while my husband was working at the boat yard. By the time my son, Victor, was four years old I was at my wit's end. Jessie, a cousin of mine who was working in the kitchen for the nuns at St. Michael's School, said they would gladly watch him in the nursery at no charge. I praised God the morning he left to go there with his father. Paul was two at the time and Madelyn was one. Then Robert Allan was born in 1953, Arthur Michael (Chuck) in 1955, and seven years later my baby, David John, in 1962. I loved every single one of them from the day of their births. They filled my life with happiness, along with my daily household chores and prayers, of course. Truthfully I never gave a thought to the strain I was under—and, of course, I did not know what was to come.

I am the vine,

and you are

the branches.

John 15:5

I have always believed in the power of the Memorare Prayer and have a deep abiding love for the Blessed Mother. Above is a photograph of her statue, which today graces the rose garden at my son Victor's home. I was very blessed to spend many hours at this special place while I wrote this book.

Chapter Five

The Memorare

It was really in the later years that things became more difficult. The young years were easier because both their father and I were disciplinarians and agreed on ground rules which, I might add, were numerous. They had to share (since they had little material things), they had to care (since they were close in age), and they had to respect one another's feelings. Of course, at times they didn't—especially Victor who was the oldest and demanded attention from us! Being the first, he was always thinking he was in charge when his dad was out working. Yet, all in all, with ground rules and the protection of God, I believed it would eventually all fall into place. I had to look on the positive side of life. We never did have enough money for food and clothing, in the way I had become accustomed to in the past, but somehow we always managed.

The basement at Oakley Street sometimes reeked of mildew and other deplorable odors. Sometimes the cesspool would emerge up onto the front yard with sewage all over the place. It was truly putrid! The garage actually leaned to one side, preventing the garage door from closing. If by some miracle it did close, it made a terrible noise! When I was unhappy, I hid my sadness and frustration from the children. I always wanted *them* to be happy and never see me being sad.

Our first home was so difficult to live in. It had only two bedrooms, and eventually four of our six children stayed all together in one of them while we lived there! Grandpa Tony Vanacore, "The Tyrant," was the most difficult to live with. He drove the children crazy, but I tolerated him because he was their grandpa. But there were times I felt like taking off my shoe and throwing it at him, too! His attitude made my husband's mother, Noni Madeline, angry too. Our poor Noni would say, "God must take him first because if I go first no one will want him." Noni Madeline died in 1950, three months after our second son, Paul, was born. She was a beautiful grandma. The kids would have loved being with her longer, but the Lord did not grant her a full life with the children.

Grandpa ended up living with us for another 15 years. The chaos grew worse because he was like another child—unruly, mean, and dominating. The moment he stepped into our kitchen, which was the first room in our apartment, he would always have to complain about the children being noisy or that their toys were thrown around in the backyard. His cane was his yardstick. He would use it the first chance he would get, to swing it at one of the children, especially young Victor. I kept thinking, "Gosh, I never did think I was going to settle for a life like this!" When I complained to my husband, he would say, "All I need is seven years and I promise we will move." I just wished for the seven years to go by quickly. I tried to cope one day at a time, but I kept losing my patience.

How can I describe my husband, the father of my children? Truthfully I don't believe they could have had a better father. He loved his mother and always felt he had an obligation to his father. As the children kept coming, he was happy and content. He worked hard and made sure they had what they needed. The children never had anything new, but he could fix anything. Being a tool maker and a mechanic, he would work on their used bicycles, ice skates, and cars. He would bring home old wagons and tires. He even brought an old bar room piano and repaired all the keys. He was a "Mr. Fix It"—and I swear he would break things just so he could fix them!

A Cry for Help on Colonial Road

The Memorarae Prayer

One day in 1953 while I was living on Oakley Street, my father needed help. Mom called me and said, "Gloria, your dad is in some sort of trouble. You must try to come right away." She wouldn't tell me anything about it on the phone. She just said, "Your father needs you!" I thought, "Now what?" I ended up taking the bus into Brooklyn and then the subway to their home on Colonial Road. I figured it had something to do with my siblings. I already knew that he did not want my sister, Fran, to marry this "perfect gentleman" that had come into her life, although I felt that he could have made her happy. Of course I knew that I needed to ease my dad's way of thinking about their relationship. Then there was my brother who wanted to marry a beautiful woman who was good for him, but she had been married before. In fact he did marry her, and as the Lord made it right, they had two beautiful daughters, Emily and Candy. So all was well with them.

I would soon realize that this incident had to be the worst that had happened after I left home. My father had been subjected to a temptation at work and had taken the bait. As I walked in, my dad was sitting in his usual maple rocking chair. He sighed and said in Italian, "Gloria, I have committed a wrong, and I am going to pay for it dearly."

I said, "Pop, what could you have done that can't be fixed?" He replied, "I stole and I will pay for it dearly. I am ashamed and I am a dishonor to myself and to my family." I replied, "Come on, Pop, it can't be that bad."

"I disgraced my home," he replied. "That darned Angelo (a fellow employee) tempted me." He told me that it was okay to take two lamps that had been sitting around in the storage warehouse for a long time He knew I had admired and wanted them for your mother. He said to put them on a truck for delivery to our home, so I decided to do as he had suggested. They would be delivered free of charge the following morning without a receipt. By the end of the work day, an order came in to cancel all merchandise going out on the truck."

My father was afraid he would be found out. My poor Papa was so sad. I tried to calm him down. I said, "Don't worry. It will be okay."

I left my father at home and went across the street to the monastery for about two hours. There was a bench in front of Our Lady, my beautiful Blessed Mother. Embedded in the bench was the Memorarae Prayer printed under a glass covering. I never did know that prayer before, but by repeating it for an hour and a half, I memorized it! I am still saying the Memorare to Our Blessed Mother today after completion of the Rosary at the El Jen Care Center.

When I returned to see my dad, he was still sitting in the identical position I left him in, with his head hung low. I walked over to him and said, "You must do as I say. I want you to take your shower, go to bed, and in the morning, go straight to work. When you arrive, walk straight to your bench and don't say one word."

I knew in my heart that my prayer to Our Lady would be answered. My father did as I suggested and later, at lunchtime, called me in amazement. He was so excited and speaking in Italian, "Daughter of mine, how did you know I was going to be free of my heavy burden?"

I told him not to worry. I had faith and I knew and trusted in Our Lady, the Blessed Mother—My Lady.

The Memorare

Remember, O most gracious Virgin Mary, that never was it known that anyone who fled to thy protection, implored thy help, or sought thy intercession was left unaided. Inspired with this confidence, I fly to thee, O Virgin of virgins, my Mother; to thee do I come; before thee I stand, sinful and sorrowful. O Mother of the Word Incarnate, despise not my petitions but in thy mercy hear and answer me.

Amen

I must admit, I never did get accustomed to life on Oakley Street. I dreaded living there. In 1956 my nephew, Anthony (Mac), asked if he could move in with us at the end of his tour of duty in the Navy. He gave me six dollars a week to make his lunch every weekday. As the children kept coming, it got even worse living in a house with only two bedrooms. Good Lord, it was a nightmare! Now that I think of it, I felt like I was in a cuckoo's nest! I thank God that I was there to care for the children. Their father Vic said I was miserable for seven years. Such was life on Oakley Street. Getting close to the seventh year of our marriage, I wondered why my husband had said, "seven years" until we would move, because it had not happened yet. It actually turned out to take ten years!

One crazy weekend I left Vic and his father, Grandpa, who was still living with us. I just couldn't handle it all anymore. I took all the children to my sister Fran's place in Long Island. I thought that could be my getaway. All five children loved it at her house, and there was no Grandpa to contend with. We stayed about a week, until Vic called and insisted we come back. He promised that Grandpa's house would soon be put up for sale and that soon we could move. Thank the Lord! I have to say that this time had been the most uncomfortable part of my life, and it was going to be the beginning of a *new* life for the children. I never thought that day would come but, then again, I believed that God did. He knew it would.

Meanwhile Vic kept working at the boat yard. On Sundays he would take the day off in order to take the children to Mass. Sometimes he would take the children to visit his elderly aunts. He also liked having his children at home to help with work, but on weekends some of them disliked being kept at home working without a break. As the ones who felt resentful began to grow older, they were yearning to get on with their lives and see their friends on weekends. Sometimes we did get my mom and dad to come to the bus station in New Haven between our visits to them. It became a much easier task for us to pick them up there than drive to Brooklyn. The children were always thrilled seeing them. My parents would arrive with shopping bags full of their favorite marshmallow cookies, other delicacies, and Italian food, which we could not afford at the time.

As the time went by, I realized that I had no choice but to just deal with my own situation. Since the children were so close in age—all playing and doing chores together, growing up in a "tribe," it was like I was bringing up an army. This was because I always gave my full attention all day long to the children and daily household chores. The children called me "The Sergeant." There we were—the children, their Grandpa Tony, me, and their dad (my husband). I felt surrounded by people but still, somewhat alone.

Yes, Victor was a great father but not the best of husbands. I must say, the children may not have thought of him as a "good dad," but I did. I called my husband "Il Duce," the "Raging Bull"—and, sometimes "Hitler" but when I look back, I wouldn't want it any other way. I don't believe they would have turned out the way they did had they not had rules and regulations to follow, such as: love and respect for one another at the top of the list, good sportsmanship, chores to do, and praying together our nightly prayer, the Rosary—with "The Tyrant."

Chapter Six
Another Dream Come True

In 1956 we traded a boat for a lot upon which we could build our new home, and in 1957 we finally sold the Oakley Street residence. We would soon move into our new, but unfinished, home at 120 Blakeslee Avenue in North Haven! It was truly "A Dream Come True!" It was the greatest deal my husband ever made. When I first saw the lot, Victor looked at me and said, "Gloria, can you picture this place a few years from now?" I suppose I didn't have any imagination at the time. I looked at him and, once again, thought he was nuts. My emotions were so mixed up. I thought, "God, is this it?" Then I said flat out, "Sorry, Vic. I see a dirty old mud-hole, an empty dirt lot, a big unfinished house, and eight people moving in." I thought again, "Is it just *me*, Lord? Do I expect too much out of life?"

I would later have to admit that it would be heaven on earth there for the children. The water I saw was *not* a "mud-hole," even though at first I thought it looked like one. In fact, it was a naturally spring-fed pond. The property had more space for them to play and have fun in without their grandpa complaining about the ruckus they made. However, we never did fully realize how much more work would have to be done.

The months and years went by. The children would grow up and would work on the house with their father every Saturday and Sunday when he was at home. He did allow them playtime, but we had them all doing special chores. They resented it because they had to follow strict rules and regulations. It was chores first and *then* playtime. If they didn't help, they didn't play. That was our motto. But the hard work was all worth the struggle. As for the grumbling, only the Lord knows what the children were thinking and saying to themselves. Even though their dad was the "Sergeant-at-Arms," they all had a piece of paradise around our home after a few years of hard work.

"The Family That Prays Together *Stays* Together"

Somehow we always managed to say our prayers in the evening. The Rosary was a nightly chore. I write "chore" because it seemed like one, since I was trying to get the children to kneel around the table and not touch the chairs. Now that I look back, it was good discipline for the children. Prayer was always a must in our home and it became a habit for the entire family. I truly believed that praying together would have the effect of what the Reverend Fulton J. Sheen often said: "The family that prays together stays together." Grandpa was the one who insisted that we all say the Rosary every night after dinner. I believe he was used to saying it with Grandma when she was alive and well. She was a very spiritual woman. Grandpa must have felt good, ordering the boys and Madelyn to kneel around the table with his cane in one hand and his Rosary in the other.

As the years went by Grandpa was getting older, and the children began to realize that he was starting to skip half of the prayers and he was repeating others. We could see that forgetfulness was setting in. My son Victor said, "Mom, I think Grandpa is going crazy; he is not saying the prayers right." I chuckled, knowing it was now time for Grandpa to give them a break. The children seemed elated. Robert, my son with the bony knees, said, "Thank God for that. My knee bones are wearing out!" I should have continued the nightly Rosary, but I didn't have the patience. I actually couldn't wait for their bedtime, so I could have time to do the other chores I couldn't get to during the day.

On the top floor we now had a large bedroom for Grandpa and one for the boys directly across from him. The boys would keep an eye on him, even though he thought he was keeping an eye on them. Our nephew, Anthony (Mac), shared the room with Grandpa, and the children just loved him being with us. How could we refuse cousin Mac! Then one day the children found a dog in the woods and named him "Duke." We couldn't have a home without a dog! He was a black Cocker Spaniel with laughing eyes and a waggling tail, who jumped up on them as if he belonged to them. How could I say no (even though their dad already had Cleo, his hunting dog, for many years)? So we ended up with five children, Grandpa, Mac, the two dogs Cleo and Duke, until we were blessed with our new baby boy, David.

The grass became greener and the pond out back was now the perfect place for the children to enjoy … I've always loved the water … the peacefulness … the restfulness and beauty … My Lord had given us … a wonderful home the children could enjoy …

Gloria Vanacore

The Pond

Our family home on Blakeslee Avenue was on a hill together with eight other houses around a pond. Ours was the only custom home. The others were split-level tract homes, all alike. At the beginning the pond had not been dredged and leveled off so all the homeowners got together and had the pond dredged, cleaned, and leveled. Now all of the children would have to learn how to swim. Then and there, I decided it was time for me to drive, so I could take them to lessons. I already had my license but had put off driving for a while. I said, "This is it! These kids are going to have to learn to swim!" They soon began swimming classes at Wharton Brook. I packed them into the car and drove them regularly.

Believe me, it was cold and dreary and we had to be there at 6 a.m. Robert was the middle child and somewhat hesitant at the time. He kept telling me he couldn't go into the water because it was too cold. I would not take "No" for an answer. I said, "You're getting in that cold water, if I have to take you in myself." I was determined they were all going to learn how to swim. We went two to three times a week, and in three months they were all swimming like fish! Paul was the strongest swimmer of them all! My heart and my mind were so relieved.

Even so, they still were not allowed to go in the pond to swim, unless I was out there watching or another adult was present. My husband also built a large raft and set it in the middle of the pond. What a wonderful playground the children had for themselves and for all of their friends. They would soon make our backyard into a baseball field, badminton court, basketball court, and then added hockey goals in the winter. In the subsequent years the trees started to grow. The grass became greener and the pond out back was now the perfect place for the children to enjoy swimming and fishing in the summer, as well as, ice skating and ice hockey in the winter. What a wonderful world the children had. My Lord had given us a fun home they could enjoy with their friends. How good this was.

As time went on our front driveway became their high school bus stop. All of their friends knew they could not go out to play ball or skate unless they had finished their share of the work. Each child continued as they got older to have their own chores. They alternated their chores and we had a big black board on the wall of our slightly finished walk-in basement where they were written. For instance, they did household chores which included: cleaning the windows, vacuuming, scrubbing the floors, bathrooms, and kitchen—including the stove, baking Bundt cakes, or doing laundry and folding the clothes. If they were not done, they did not go outside or to the pond.

The children entertained themselves well and kept busy. They were not allowed to sit around doing nothing. They were never bored and always had something to do. They practiced their instruments and played indoor games. Yes, we had a television, but it did not seem to distract them. They were too busy with their homework, household duties, and playing outdoors. It always seemed like a big, bustling, energetic playground at our home. I did not mind it either, except for the fact that most of the house itself remained unfinished. Knobs still had to be put on doors and some rooms still had to be painted The basement also had to be finished. My husband even put clips on the knobs of our old hand-me-down TV, instead of replacing them. He was already putting in a lot of hours, working at his boatyard, and would say that everything at home was "done for now," That was one of his favorite expressions. Oh yes, naturally being a woman I complained, but after a while I got so used to it that I lived with it.

All I knew was that the children were happy—and that was all that mattered. Their friends were happy too. Those were the fun "growing-up" years. If children in the neighborhood wanted to use the pond in wintertime, my husband told them they would have to help out with some chores, alongside my children, to get this privilege. For example, in order to play hockey they had to shovel our driveway and the pond. In order to play basketball and baseball, they had to help my children mow the lawn.

Their dad never *did* show his emotions, but I eventually realized that he really cared about us. It was simply that he never did *express* his feelings one way or the other. Our children grew up healthy, happy, and well adjusted. Like every other child, they had their moments of frustration. Show me *one* child who doesn't have those! Somehow I knew they would get over it. I called it a combination of discipline and gut instinct.

Looking back, I feel that my miracles in this life really began while we were living in our home on Blakeslee Avenue. But in those days I never did realize what a gift from heaven our home on Blakeslee Avenue was. Who ever dreamed the children could have this beautiful location to live in? They were truly blessed.

The Assumption of the Blessed Mother

Assumption Day is on August 15th every year. It is a day I have always held very dearly in my heart as a time for prayer and reflection. I believe it was also a day of divine intervention in the young life of Victor Jr.

Thank You My Lord!

Chapter Seven

Many Stories To Tell

Gifts and Blessings

What doesn't happen with children growing up? What names can I give the stories in this chapter? Incidents? Gifts? Moral Lessons? Blessings? Miracles? Here are some of those special moments with a few stories, later on, that will give you a chuckle too …

Assumption Day 1958

In August we had a family picnic with friends at Fort Hale Park, not far from New Haven. It was so successful that on the following day, a Monday, we decided to have another picnic, since there was so much food left over. This was always the case—all of us being of Italian descent. Spending so much time together with our families was so much fun, with a lot of laughter. A poker game was always included too. That Monday morning it had been difficult to get everything done in our busy household. As we were getting ready, as hectic as it was, I had realized that it was August 15th Assumption Day, a day I held very dearly for prayer and meditation. Something in the back of my mind kept telling me to at least pay a visit to my Blessed Mother that day. I had a sudden urge to just jump in the car and go. For some strange reason, I looked at Vic Jr. again who was always "the handful" of the bunch, somewhat of a troublemaker with a strong mind of his own. I said, "Vic, you're coming with me for a short visit to church!"

He gave me a crazy look and said, "Why me, Mom?"

I said, "Don't give me an argument. Get into the car. This won't take long." Somehow I just felt I had to take him and go! I also insisted that he wear a belt that day to keep his trousers up. Even though he refused, I made him put one on anyway to visit Blessed Mother. When we arrived at St. Barnabas Church, we walked directly to Our Lady. No Mass was going on. I knelt down with Vic and said, "Please, my Lady, watch over him. This one needs it. He does get wild at times and is always getting into some sort of mischief. Please watch over Victor and all of the children. Blessed Mother, I love you so much."

Little did I know what was to occur on that very day. When we arrived home, I soon received some unexpected company. In came my cousin Tut, his wife, and four children, who were all on their way to Cape Cod. They were going to spend five days on vacation at a family resort and had decided to stop by our home on the way. Now *all* of us were so excited, since the children were all about the same age. Seeing the big backyard and the pond, Tut shouted, "This looks like a lot of fun!" One of Tut's children asked their father and mother, "Why can't we stay here? We could have more fun with our cousins."

My cousin looked at me and said, "What do you think, Cuz? Could we handle this bunch? Do you mind if we stay here instead? My kids would love this fun place. You have the pond, a baseball field, and a badminton net—all the comforts for fun and relaxation! I'm willing to pay there for one month but stay here for one week."

Gosh, it was like a gift! Loving my children and seeing their happy faces and the family all together—how could I refuse? "Cuz" went out and purchased a beach umbrella, chairs, and some water toys. He filled up the fridge with all kinds of food and drinks. Then his family and our friends all came along on the picnic that we had planned for the day near the shore. Little did I know that Cuz was soon going to be my hero! Over the course of the day, we had our picnic lunch with all the leftovers from the day before. The children were having a wonderful time. Then suddenly, while we were playing our card game, one of the men in our group ran toward us looking very pale, yelling, "Hurry, we need help. Young Vic is *HANGING OFF THE CLIFF BY HIS BELT ON A BRANCH!* It looks like he is going to fall!"

We all ran toward the cliff. We could not see him but I heard a little voice saying, "Don't worry, Mom. It is not bad. When the tide comes in I can jump." It was Vic who was only 10 years old at that time. Who in heaven knew when the tide would come in, let alone know how long that branch would last. I kept thanking God that he had worn the belt I had insisted he wear to hold up his trousers. Little did I know that his belt would catch on the branch as he slid down the cliff—and ***HELP SAVE HIS LIFE!***

We all approached the cliff. It started to drizzle and became cloudy. I thought, "Lord, it is getting dark! Now what?" The ambulance, police, and fire department came. A crowd gathered in the park—all watching! All I could do was to kneel down and start praying. I implored, "Lord! Only You can save him!"

Tut, who was the strongest of the men, decided to take action first. He grabbed the fire hose, threw it down, and tied a rope around our uncle Tony, my husband's older brother, who was one of the men in our group. He did not want to trust the fire department. Tony was a retired Naval Officer with special training and I trusted him *completely*. They lowered him down. Then Tony tied a rope around young Vic and brought him up. He was bruised with a shirt tattered and torn, but he came up safely. For the moment I hugged him, but at the same moment I wanted to slap him for getting everyone so upset and scared.

This was a moment of divine intervention. Little did I realize that it was the beginning of the many miracles that I would receive as my journey of life continued.

Thank you, my Lord, for being there for us!

Vanacores Don't Lie

One evening while Victor and I went to a meeting, Victor Jr. (14) and Paul (12) decided to take a trial run with the family car. It was parked at the end of our circular driveway. Robert, who was only 9, jumped in the back seat. Well, lo and behold, they drove the car from the back of the house and around the circular driveway. Then they turned around and the car rolled right into the concrete wall right next to our house. Then they left the car there and ran inside. When we arrived home that evening, the first thing their father noticed was where the car was and the damage to it. He shouted, "Holy Smokes! What happened to the car?" Victor ran into the house like a raging bull and called the children to come downstairs. He demanded to know what happened, but by then the boys had conjured up their story. They told him that someone had come into the driveway and driven the car down into the wall.

Their dad said, "Are you sure you're telling me the truth?" They answered, "Yes, Dad, it's true."

He said, "Well, then I have to call the police department and give them a report." He picked up the phone, called the police, and reported the incident to them.

When the children went up to bed that night, they couldn't sleep. They began to think it over. Then, by either conscience or fear, they decided—then and there—to go directly back downstairs, wake up their father, tell him they had lied, and that the accident was their fault.

At that moment, their father went ballistic. He sat down, put his face in his hands, and cried, "I can't believe you lied to me! How could you do this? I am mortified!" He never before had believed that they would be capable of pulling this stunt. Then he picked up the phone and told the police to cancel the report. "I am ashamed to tell you this, but the children lied to us," he said.

Of course the children were grounded—no television, no friends over, and all games were canceled for two weeks. Before long, I felt punished too. I couldn't stand them all together in the house. After some persuasion on my part, their punishment lasted 12 days. They went out into the backyard and proceeded to repair the damage they had caused to the car and to the wall. The children never lied after that.

Chuck Loses the Tip of His Finger

One day the children's aunt Renee decided to take them to a movie. They all got in the car and Chuck was the last one to get in. Aunt Renee, being in a hurry, did not see Chuck's little hand and slammed the door on his finger. It was hanging by a thread. She came in quickly, rushing with him toward the sink. I saw the blood. By the grace of God, I grabbed a white towel from the counter and saw the severity of his injury. We jumped into the car again. Thank God, my doctor was there getting his mail out of the mailbox. He saw me in a panic and said, "This is my day off, Mrs. Vanacore. I just stopped in to get my mail.

I shouted at him, "Well, Doctor, you will have to get to work. This is an emergency! My son's finger is coming off. Please!" I begged.

Of course he opened his office door and we went in. Chuck was crying. I had done all the screaming for him. Doctor Feinberg wrapped him in a clean sheet clean in preparation for surgery. He also told me to call my husband to get an okay for emergency treatment. When he was finished, and had bandaged Chuck's injury, the doctor said, "He is not the piano player, is he? But don't worry, the scar will heal and his finger will be as good as new." I just thank God the doctor was there. when I needed him, almost as if he was waiting for me near his mailbox—even though it was his day off! *Thank God, again!*

Hidden Halloween Candy

I think that all children look forward to Halloween night, and it was a big treat, of course, for our children. In our daily life CANDY WAS NOT ALLOWED! Nor were Oreo cookies and the like. Sweets were a "no-no." However, ice cream was a *Yes!* That was their treat. So of course when Halloween came, the children, hoping for some treats, would think, "This is our night!" For years I had never allowed them to go trick-or-treating alone. I felt they were too young. One Halloween night they begged me, "It's not fair, Mom. We want to go out with our friends." So they went with a group of neighborhood children and their parents. I agreed to it. They would begin at sundown.

By the time their dad was home from work, they had returned, bringing home enough chocolates, lollipops, and apples to fill a large crate. My husband, as he always had done, started to empty out their pillow cases; we could not afford to buy bags for them at the time. In the past he had always separated the chocolates into two bowls: M&Ms, Hershey Bars, Mounds, and all the *good* chocolates in the first bowl, and the *lesser quality* junk, sugary sweets aside in the second bowl, telling them, "This is not good for your teeth and we can't afford a dentist."

They would always look at him with a collective expression of disappointment and disgust. *In fact*, their father and grandfather would always eat all the good candy in front of the television and give out the junk candy to the "trick-or-treaters" who came after the children got home. All that would be left for our children would be the apples. Well, that particular Halloween was the last straw! This had gone on for several years. The children had already gathered for a meeting upstairs, before that evening, and decided to "fix" Dad. They would often have "meetings" upstairs to talk things over. They had made a plan.

They had taken neckties and bed sheets, attached them together, made a rope and tied it around the handle of a galvanized bucket. Our oldest son, Victor Jr., had arrived home before the rest of the children and said he had to use the bathroom upstairs. He ran upstairs to the boys' bedroom, which was on the side of the house, to lower the bucket. Paul, Madelyn, Robert and Chuckie were already waiting at the bottom, separating some of the good candy and placing it in the bucket. Victor Jr. would then slowly and quietly raise the bucket up to the second floor to empty it. That night they all continued lifting and lowering the bucket until there were just a few good candies left in the pillow cases to avoid suspicion. Chuck was standing beside Madelyn and Robert, ready to bring the less good candy into the house. They would later hide their empty candy wrappers behind the coil heaters in their grandpa's second floor bedroom.

That first year, after they were on to their dad's tactics, Victor looked into their bags to separate the good candy from the junk candy and said, "Hey, Gloria, they're sure getting cheap this year. There's only a few pieces of chocolate here and the rest are all lollipops and apples." The children's plan had worked! This continued for another two years. Then on one cold winter night after Halloween, Grandpa decided to see if he could get more heat in the bathroom. He started to knock on the radiator and, lo and behold, out came a storm of chocolate candy wrappers from behind. Oh God! Here came another "Vanacore Scenario!" Grandpa shouted, "Vic! You think your kids are angels now? Come up here!" My husband went upstairs. Showing him all the wrappers, Grandpa said, "*They* were the culprits who ate all the good candy!"

Downstairs the kids all smirked with sly grins. "We fixed them!" they thought silently. I believe that was the last of the Halloween escapades. By then the children were all too old to go out trick-or-treating. (P.S. from a "Proud Mom": they all ended up with perfect teeth.) No braces were needed and all of them had beautiful smiles, thanks to "rules and regulations." Maybe some of the "apples only" trick-or-treat nights actually helped after all!

"Not Guilty!"—a Halloween Verdict!

On one other Halloween evening, the children were accused of breaking the mailbox of my next door neighbor. On the contrary, I believed that my children, in particular, just bothered her. She did not have children of her own, so of course she always had a complaint. The Vanacore boys, it seems, were always the cause of her complaints, *most of the time!* So the following Halloween, as a precaution, I kept them home, as if I knew a complaint would happen again. Sure enough, there was a fire in a nearby barn and the owner found an I.D. bracelet with Victor Jr.'s name on it.

Naturally, the police came knocking at the door! I was waiting for some sort of reprimand. I was only too happy to reply, "Sorry, Officer, you've come to the wrong place. I can prove to you that my children were all here last night." Victor Jr. was also quick to explain to the officer that the previous summer, he had lost the Identification "ID" .bracelet his grandmother gave him and had not wanted to tell anyone.

As the children grew older, it became harder for both my husband Vic and me. Thank God for Vic! He was stern and that was the way I wanted it. I was stern also, but he *never* backed down on a punishment they deserved. Now and then, I would want to give in, especially when I really knew they were sorry for what they had done.

Chapter Eight

Why Now God?

In 1960 my youngest son, Chuck, started to go to school. This was a day I had awaited for many years. Having all five children in school was such a great new experience for me. I could now see the light at the end of the tunnel! Finally, I could go to work and earn some extra money. At the time Vic Jr. was taking music lessons with Sister Marjorie at St. Mary's High School. I could help pay for his music lessons, food for the family, and for the weekly poker games I enjoyed with friends. I read an ad in the newspaper for a part-time position at J.C. Penny's department store in Hamden, Connecticut and thought they might hire me. The work hours would be from 9 a.m. to 3 p.m. When I went in for the interview, I asked if it was at all possible to work from 9 a.m. to 2 p.m. so I could be home before the kids got back from school, hoping they would understand. Instead I was told, "No such hours. It had to be 9 a.m. to 3 p.m." That was it, and there was no other way. Absolutely not! I wanted my children to find me at home.

As I was walking out of the office disappointed, the supervisor was walking in. I gave him a smile, not knowing who he was, and he asked if I got the job. I said, "No such luck! I would have to work until 3 p.m. and it is impossible for me. I have a bunch of kids in school and I need to be home earlier." Luckily he responded with a big smile and said, "Come on in. That won't be a problem." I was hired that *very* day!

I was so happy at how everything seemed to fall into place. It was just great! I felt like a million dollars – like I was floating on air! I don't remember my exact salary, but I felt *so* good, buying extra food and paying for music lessons. Even though I started there part-time, I also received a store discount and was able to buy the children their clothes on sale. *And*—I had finally got my shape back again, after being pregnant all those years! There was not a day that I didn't thank the Lord for his gifts. It seemed my prayers had worked one more time, and I always thanked the Lord *every* time.

My new life only lasted two years. Then *Oops—a bombshell hit me!* I became pregnant again! "Another baby, God? Again, God?" I gasped, "This cannot happen to me. Not again! I'm 38 years old! Oh, My Lord, please—not now!" Poor Sister Marjorie at St. Mary's High School had to hear me, anxious and upset again. I spoke to her about my pregnancy and told her how disappointed I was. I remember I was having a good cry. Of course, her response was *so* positive and sweet. She held my hand and replied in her gentle voice, "Now, Mrs. Vanacore, don't fret or feel badly. Children are a joy! This baby will give you *great* joy. Your older ones will 'fly the coop' (as she put it), be grown and on their own and you will still have *this* one. You will never be lonely. and he or she will be a comfort to you – I promise you. And furthermore," she continued, "*I* will get a chance to teach *this* child music and you may have another genius on your hands! You will have another musician who you will be proud of. You never know what the Lord has in store. He has His reasons. Someday Vic and his younger sibling will be working and playing piano together."

Well, Sister Marjorie's words came true. Little did I realize then, how right she was! I gave birth to a baby boy who I named David in 1962. I must admit, to my surprise, my heart just jumped when I saw him for the first time. To me he had the face of an angel. And, bringing up David was easier than I thought it would be. The other children were older and were thrilled with the thought of having a baby brother. Our baby, David, was adored and watched over by his siblings with endearing love and affection. He started his music lessons at age six. At the time his older brother, Vic Jr., was in the Navy and playing in the Navy Band. I do believe in my heart, the Lord sent David to me for a reason.

Paul's Water Skiing Accident
Madelyn's Faith: *Yes, he is!*

As teenagers, one day in about 1965, the children decided to go water skiing with some friends at Lake Zoar in Connecticut. Apparently when it was Paul's turn to ski, he put on a life belt and a ski and took off. Every time the boat would go into a turn, he leaned into the turn then pulled on a rope. When he did this, it doubled his speed. There was a lot of boat traffic that day. As Paul got too close to the back of a passing boat on the lake, he hit their wake, went flying through the air, and landed on his stomach. This knocked the wind right out of him. A piece of gum he was chewing also managed to get logged in his throat! At the time they didn't yet have water skiing vests, and the belt Paul was wearing did nothing more than keep him afloat with his head still submerged in the water!

When they finally pulled Paul back into the boat, they rushed back to the shore. Someone covered him up. A man on the beach looked at my son and predicted, "He's too far gone. He's not going to make it."

His sister, Madelyn, had faith in the Lord and said, "Yes he is!" They quickly turned Paul over and pushed on his back. The gum came out of his mouth, but he still remained unconscious. He was turning blue, and no one there knew how to resuscitate him. An ambulance was called and Paul was taken to Griffin's Hospital, an hour's drive away. While Madelyn and her brothers chased the ambulance all the way to the hospital, they prayed aloud together in the car.

At the time my husband, Victor, and I were at home sitting in our backyard with our neighbors. I heard the phone ring in the house. Honestly, I immediately felt something coming over me. I said to Vic, "I have a feeling that something happened to Paul." Yet I thought to myself, "Why Paul?" There were so many friends with them. At that moment my heart kept throbbing, as I ran into the house and picked up the phone. It was a nurse at Griffin's Hospital informing me that Paul and his friends were on their way home. He had swallowed too much water when he fell. After the hospital resuscitated him he was released. Because he was not of age, by law they had to notify me that they had resuscitated him. He was going to be fine.

Thank you, Lord—again, for being there.

My Miracle Phone Call from Viet Nam

Hail Mary, Full of Grace …

I should have known then and there, how much
My Lady, the Mother of My Lord, meant to me …

In 1968 my son Paul joined the Navy Reserves. Never in a million years did I ever dream that Paul would end up in active service in Vietnam War zones where he could be killed at any moment. After he went overseas, the time soon arrived when I hadn't heard from him for weeks. I was seeing disastrous events overseas on the news every day. My mind was in turmoil going around in circles. My heart would take an extra beat every time I walked to the mailbox or heard the phone ring, "Where could he be? Why haven't I heard from him?" I would search the television news broadcasts and newspapers. All the boys looked the same in the news photos. Their faces were always camouflaged. One time I even thought that one of those faces resembled Paul. I just wanted to believe he was still alive! I would say the "Hail Mary" and pray, "God, please protect him!"

Hail Mary, full of grace, the Lord is with thee.
Blessed art thou among women, and
blessed is the Fruit of Thy Womb, Jesus.
Holy Mary, Mother of God, pray
for us sinners, Now, and
at the hour of our death.
... Amen

One special morning I noticed a listing of the movie *Our Lady of Fatima* in the TV guide. It was going to be on at 7 p.m. It was not as if I had never seen it before. I remembered that Linda Darnell played the part of Our Lady. Who could forget that movie! It was one of my favorite films. I loved seeing it, time and again. For those who are unfamiliar with Our Lady of Fatima, she is synonymous with the Blessed Virgin Mary. In 1917 three shepherd children saw apparitions of her at Fatima, Portugal. She imparted three important secrets to them. Thousands of visitors travel to her shrine every year.

That evening I thought I would try to have some peace and quiet, so I went upstairs to watch and pray by myself while my husband and children watched it in the basement. Victor Jr. was on leave from the military that week and happened to be home. He decided to join me upstairs for some quiet time. I put the "Our Lady of Fatima" movie on television for the children. After seeing the film so many times before, I knew exactly when the Blessed Mother was going to appear to the three shepherd children. I knelt down immediately and pleaded, "My dear Blessed Mother. Please! I beg you to let me hear from my son, Paul. I am so afraid he will never come home" … and, sure enough, at that very moment my phone rang!

My son, Victor, jumped up to answer the phone and held it to his ear with a look of amazement. I felt I was in a trance. In a shaky voice Victor called out, "Mom, quick come here. You won't believe this. It is an 'S.O.S.' collect call from a ham radio operator in Long Beach, California! I quickly got off of my knees and ran to the phone. The operator's voice came out deeply and clear. He said, "Ma'am, are you Mrs. Vanacore?" "Yes," I replied.

He said, "Ma'am, I am relaying a call from Paul Vanacore." I asked immediately, "Is he okay?"

"Hold it. He doesn't have much time," he cautioned. "Do not ask him where he is. He wants to tell you that he is okay. Just say 'OVER,' and then you can tell him, 'All is okay here.' Please do not ask questions. You have one minute." I did as the operator asked, had a good cry, and thanked my Blessed Mother for coming through for me.

Well it was all I needed to believe that Paul was all right and under the Lord's protection. I cried, "Yes!" Truthfully at the time I was excited, but it still didn't sink in. There was so much going on. I was perplexed. The days went on my love for Our Lord grew stronger. There is a *Faith* that is more precious than all of the treasures on this earth! *Faith Is More Precious Than Gold!*

Here I am with my sons in 1969. Paul went into the U.S. Navy and had the misfortune of serving in the Vietnam War. Who could ever forget Paul's "S.O.S." phone call to me! Or Victor's "AWOL," when he called out for me!

May God Bless and Protect Our Country and Those Who Serve

Chapter Nine

Heaven Whispers

Victor gone A.W.O.L.?

One morning while I was going in to work at Zurich Insurance Company, I noticed a sign on one of the office doors. It read "Psychic Course 6:00 to 8:00 p.m.: begins Monday to Friday next week." Naturally I thought to myself, "This is great!" It was sure something I wanted to look into, since I had always been curious about the "sixth sense." There were times when I sensed that I actually did have it, especially where my children were concerned. I thought, "Why not! What do I have to lose?" Interesting? Certainly! Exciting? Yes!

I walked into the first class session and told the instructor that I would like to take the course. She asked me why. I explained that I had strange feelings about premonitions. She looked at my hand and said, "Oh yes! I can see that you would be a good candidate for this!" After questioning all of the other students that walked in, she began the class. A few minutes later she said, "There's going to be an accident on the street outside." Lo and behold! About five minutes later, there was a car accident—just as she had predicted.

In the class I was taught that I had to be aware, and to write notes specifying times, dates and places, as things were happening around me, both in my mind and in my dreams. I actually never followed through on writing notes. I just tried to keep things in my head. The Lord has blessed me with a remarkable memory, and I still remember happenings as clear as day. Well, I must admit that this particular course was an interesting experience. When I took classes in school, I had never found them as interesting as this one course! I just thanked God that Vic never did ask what I did with the money I earned. I guess he knew I would spend it wisely. At that time I did, since we still had some of the children living with us.

The course helped me realize that I did have another sense. I never realized at that time, how much I loved My Lord and my enduring faith in *He* who strengthened me. However, I had begun to have a feeling, at some point in my life, that I had extra-sensory perception. Today I now believe that The Lord is actually my *deep inner* sixth sense. Could that be true? I am still asking myself. Why do I have these feelings? Who am I? What is it that gives me these strange senses that I feel happening before or after an incident? It doesn't feel normal.

Victor Jr.'s AWOL Day 1967

After his graduation from high school in 1966, my son Victor Jr. applied for college music scholarships. I prayed that he would be accepted into a music college of his choice. He applied to the Navy's School of Music in Virginia and was accepted immediately. He called me from the base and said, "I'm in the Navy now!" As The Lord would have it, for him and for me, it was a gift from heaven. He was in the Navy Music School for four years. After completing his studies, he became Music Director of the Navy Band and toured the Mediterranean with them. As luck would have it, one day back at the base, Victor Jr. decided to drive off of base with a few of his fellow Navy friends without permission. That same morning at home, I woke up from a dream, hearing Victor shout, "Mom, Mom!" Immediately I knew that something had happened to him. It was about 8:30 a.m. on a Saturday morning.

I jumped out of bed and called out to Madelyn. I shouted, "Matt! Something has happened to your brother Victor!" Of course Madelyn tried to ease my mind, telling me not to worry. I told her to run to the mailbox and see if he had written to me. So Madelyn ran to the mailbox and, yes, there was a letter there from Victor. He mentioned in the letter that he would be going away for the weekend with some of his friends. I did not accept that explanation for my feeling of angst. I said, "This happened this very morning. I'm calling your Uncle Tony!" Tony was a petty officer in the Naval Reserves and could certainly find out for me, because I still felt, somehow, that Victor was in trouble."

I called Tony immediately. When I told him that I felt Victor was in trouble, he replied, "Gloria, don't worry. The parents are the first people to be notified in case of an emergency." So then I felt at ease.

The following Monday when Uncle Tony and my husband arrived at work, there was a call from Victor Jr. from the Bethesda Naval Hospital in Maryland. He told his father that he had been in a car accident over the previous weekend! He had fractured his groin and pelvis and had scratched-up hands but was otherwise fine. His friends had abandoned him, and he had been left alone in the car. None of them were hurt, but he would have to stay in the hospital, recovering for two months.

His father called me with a strange expression in his voice. "Gloria, you were right," he said. "Something *did* happen to Vic Jr., but there is no need to worry. He is fine."

I replied, "I don't believe it! He is hurting. I am going to go visit him myself."

"Don't do anything," his father said to me. "I will be coming home after work, and we will call him. You can talk to him personally then." I agreed, hung up the phone, hurriedly grabbed young David, put him in the car, and rushed to church. I went in and prayed.

After quite a while, I returned home. Then my husband drove in the driveway, and the first thing he did was to call Bethesda Hospital. He handed me the phone and said, "Speak to him yourself. He will tell you that he is okay." Victor Jr. then reassured me that he was fine, that I should not worry, and that he would be up and around soon. I had to ask him, "Victor, tell me one thing. What were you doing at 8:30 a.m. on Saturday morning?"

He remembered clearly. "I called out to you. I was hurting because they moved me from the local hospital into Bethesda Naval Hospital." Hearing him say that, I knew right then that my psychic course had worked!

A Day at the Race Track
"Luck Be A Lady!"

The week before we went to the race track, both Vic Jr. and Paul were already planning their wedding dates (against my better judgment I might add). The dates they chose were too close together for my liking. I was concerned about the expense, and I felt that they were both too young to get married. If that was not enough, I had been suffering from a terrible toothache—even *more* expense ahead! I hadn't been to the dentist for years. I always felt that it was not as important for me as it was for the children. Although the thought of going wasn't very pleasant, I went to the dentist that week. He gave me a sedative for the toothache but told me I didn't have a choice; I would need to have a root canal. I was beside myself. Gosh, I thought, "How can I do this?" I was so fed up with financial pressures. I decided to walk into church and cry it out. As God was my witness, I did not plead for money. I never prayed for money.

In desperation I thought, "My God, I've had it! My teeth are a mess. My sons want to get married. It seems so impossible. What am I going to do?" Then I cried some more.

Eventually I got over my crying and went home. That night my husband, Victor, came home from a meeting he'd had at the Knights of Columbus, a men's service group in Catholic churches. He calmly said to me, "Gloria, the Knights of Columbus are having a bus trip up to the racetrack at Green Mountain. He knew how much I would enjoy going. It was a treat to go, now and then. But I looked at him and said, "God, Vic! Right now I can't see straight, let alone go to the track. My teeth are a mess, and the boys are getting married. My heart isn't in it."

"Listen," my husband replied, "sixty dollars is not going to make a difference, and I already reserved two seats." Much to my regret, I felt I did not have a choice, because when Victor made up his mind, I always went along with him! We set off on the trip that Sunday. Believe me, this was going to be *one* heck of a bus ride, and I was not looking forward to it. We all met that morning in the church parking lot. The members and their wives were having coffee and doughnuts. When we joined them, they asked me what was wrong because, to them, I seemed too quiet and looked unhappy. I admitted that I really didn't care to go. I didn't feel right. My being there just didn't make sense. I had too much on my mind, aside from the fact that I needed a root canal.

When we arrived at the track, I mentioned to Vic that I did not want to sit where we had to climb steps. I wanted to sit closer to the track. So we sat in a section that was further down, apart from the others. We bet on the first three races but did not win any of them. In the next race, I decided to pick my mom's age. She was 74 and I was 47. So I played a "Perfecta" in which the winning ticket of a race cannot be cashed out. It has to be played on the *following* race. I had played 7-4 and, lo and behold, 7 and 4 came in! I had won! Yet, I was so upset because my winnings had to be bet on the next race. "Why do they do that?" I thought. "That's not fair."

Some men came up to me and asked to buy my ticket for 100 dollars. Another man came over and offered me 200 dollars. I asked him what it was worth, if I won the next race. He looked at me and explained, "It depends. You could lose the ticket altogether, but who knows?" I wondered about it some more and said to my husband (similar to what *he* had said to *me* a few days earlier), "What is one or two hundred dollars. Vic—shall we take a chance? We need money for the weddings and my teeth are a mess. Let's play 2 and 6."

The race began and horse number two was way ahead. Watching this, I cried aloud, "He is going to get tired. He'll never make it." Oh Gosh! I remember that the horse's name was "Lucky Kelly #2." Today I can just still see that scoreboard! Although Number #2 had been way ahead, the other horses were close behind, all bunched together. But when they came in—they were nose to nose! It was a photo finish! I shouted, "Blessed Mother!" I swear I must have sounded crazy. People around me said, "Why is she yelling 'Blessed Mother'? There's no jockey or horse named that! There's no such name." Believe me, shouting "Blessed Mother" was not a prayer. As I said earlier, I never prayed for money. I prayed for HELP!

We waited for the results. I screamed, "I know that Number #6 came in right behind Number #2," and I had played 2 and 6! I got a chill. My husband ran up to the cash window to confirm that I had won and collected my winnings. That race paid me $4,682.00!!! I was amazed. Really and truly, I felt our gift came to us from my prayers to the Blessed Mother, and what a gift it was! We paid in full for both of the weddings—*and* for my root canal!

So ... do you BELIEVE *too?*

To one who has faith,
no explanation is necessary.
To one without faith
no explanation is possible.

Saint Thomas Aquinas
1225-1274

The Passing of My Mother 1976

. I don't exactly remember when Mom's health started to go downhill. It began with her heart. I remember that she needed angina pills. She also had arthritis, but she never complained. I kept visiting her after I was married, especially after Dad died. The first weekend of February, in 1976, I visited my mom in New York with my sister, Fran. We were always so happy to be together and had so much fun. My mother just loved playing Bingo and had all of her little lucky charms with her. She would joke about it and say, "I don't understand this. With all these charms I never win." That day we all went to play Bingo, and she was in for a big surprise. One number was all that she needed for the Jackpot. She was scrambling her charms on her Bingo papers. Finally, she sat on her Bingo card. That was one of her good luck quirks. She said, "This is my address—'69'—I can't believe it!"

Well, sure enough, the caller shouted, "O-69!" Her face lit up like a Christmas tree. I was afraid she would have a heart attack. I swear she never looked so happy. She kept repeating, "I can't believe it! I can't believe it. This never happens to me!" We laughed with joy just seeing her cheerful expression. It was a Jackpot. She won $500! You would think she had won a million dollars. She had spent thousands of dollars playing Bingo for years and had never won, up until that day. God bless her.

Our weekend was fun and my sister and I returned to her home in Long Island. My son Chuck called and told me he would pick me up. Of course I was delighted. I wanted to take home the extra goodies and items I had purchased. Chuck drove 2 ½ hours to pick me up. We were about two miles from my home, when we encountered an orange cone in the middle of the road. The car before us had avoided it. We did the same but suddenly our car skidded, as we swerved around the cone, and began to roll. I grabbed my son's right arm, entwined my arm in his, and shouted, "Blessed Mother, be with us now!" Our car turned over twice and landed on the shoulder of the road, upside down. I felt no doubt that this would be my last breath of life.

I was frightened for Chuck, too. We were hanging upside down. He immediately kicked the driver's side door out, then stood up, and ran around and pulled me out of the car. I was shaken. I remember how a line of cars stopped behind us. A man rushed over to us and said, "I am a doctor. Do you need any help?" I said no, and thanked the Lord and my Blessed Mother that we did not need one. All we needed was the Intercession of Our Lady. The kind doctor drove us home in his car. Chuck's car was totaled. When we arrived back to my home, I ran in and shouted to my family, "*There IS a Blessed Mother!* She was *right there!*" That was February 9, 1976. I could not talk for two days and did not want to go anywhere, not even to the store. But I finally got the courage to get into my car and drive to church to thank My Lady.

I knelt down and thanked her with my whole heart and soul. I prayed, "I know you heard me, My Lady, and I thank you for saving my son's life. For some reason deep down inside of me, I know I must give you something back. Whatever it is, it will be God's will. I will accept anything." I was so grateful. I was able to drive and able to put the accident in the back of my mind. I kept thanking My Lord constantly. Then, two weeks later, after taking communion at Sunday Mass, I came down and sat in the pew next to my husband and whispered, *"I think something happened to my mother."* He replied, "There you go again. Don't be so paranoid."

He drove us home and as we came into the driveway, I heard the phone ring. I ran to the phone and sure enough, it was my brother-in-law, Joe. Very softly he said, "Your mom had a slight heart attack while she was attending Mass at Mother Cabrini's Chapel. My heart just sank! I knew right then and there that my mom was on her way to heaven. When we arrived at the hospital, I ran into the Intensive Care Unit. The nurse said my mother could hear me, but she was unable to speak. When I was next to her, she looked at me. I told her she would be okay and handed her my Rosary. Her last words to me were, "Gloria, take care of your brother." It was Sunday, February 22, 1976.

The nurse told us she needed rest and that we could all leave. We left the hospital and drove to my mother's home. It was a cold night. Fran and I were so exhausted that we went directly to bed. For some reason it seemed natural that Fran went into Mom's guest bedroom and that I went into Mom's bedroom. It was *so* cold. In those days the landlord turned the heating off at 10 p.m. and brought it back on at 5 a.m. In the middle of my deep sleep, I had a dream: *A large, bright hand with flames around all five fingers came rushing toward my face like a bolt of lightning* and immediately woke me up! I jumped out of bed and looked at the clock. It was 6:20 a.m.

I ran to the phone and called the hospital. I asked them what my mother's condition was. They told me she was resting comfortably, so I accepted their response.

That Monday morning, we went directly to the hospital. The nurse told us to go get a cup of coffee and wait for the doctor to come down. Right then and there, I knew that my mom had passed on. When the doctor walked in, he said, "I'm so sorry, Mrs. Vanacore. Your Mom passed away this morning." I asked, "Doctor, what was the exact time?" He answered, "6:20 a.m." A coincidence? I don't think so. It was not a shock to me. I knew in my heart that it was time to give up my mom. All I knew was that I had to accept God's will. It was time for her to leave her beautiful life, one that she enjoyed and lived so gracefully.

After my mother passed, I felt lost but unafraid. I realized I had to go on, although a part of me went with her. I had children and I had to be strong for them. They were just beginning their adult lives.

Thank you, Mom, for the care, love, and kindness you surrounded me with.

Chapter Ten

California Here We Come!

We made our move to California in 1976. My husband's company had moved to Vermont and by then, Madelyn, Victor, Paul, and Robert had all migrated to Southern California to start new lives. My daughter, Madelyn had called Victor Jr. and Paul and convinced them that Los Angeles would be the place for them. They would have more work opportunities. She told Victor Jr. that he would be wasting his musical talent and time, if he didn't move there. This eventually influenced our decision to move. It seemed that it was inevitable. We felt we must leave Connecticut to be with the children.

So we sold the home on Blakeslee Avenue and moved to California. My husband, Victor, drove across the country with our two youngest sons, Chuck and David. After I drove over with the last piece of our furniture to give to our friends in Boston, I followed by plane. Even then I asked my Lord, still questioning my existence and my mission in life, "What am I doing?" To me it seemed like I was migrating to a foreign land.

We moved into the Pine Tree Apartments in Torrance, California, and lived there for the first six months. It wasn't easy at the time. The apartment was small and it lacked privacy. I felt very confined. I missed my friends in North Haven, along with the life to which I had been accustomed. It didn't take long for us to purchase a place of our own in the San Fernando Valley in 1977 where we would live for about eight years. We bought a new home in Mission Hills on Saloma Avenue near Sepulveda Blvd. for $50,000. After we moved in, even though we were now in our own home, I really felt like I was still in a state of confusion, trying to figure it all out. I wondered what was in store for me.

One morning I came out of church, sat in the car, and began crying. A woman dressed in all white came up and knocked on my car window. "Are you all right?" she asked.

"I'm so fed up," I replied, still crying.

The woman in white said to me, "Say three Hail Mary's. It will be all right." I did what she told me to do and then I drove home.

Now that I recall, those years living in California made *no* significant difference in my life. All I know and remember is that it was a place I had to be at that time.

In 1978 we had been in our home for about a year when my husband had his first heart attack, just as I thought we were getting settled. I thought, "Lord, this couldn't happen. Not now!" I now felt that we were really in "no man's land." We didn't know a doctor in California or even know of a hospital close to us! I thought quickly to myself that the "Yellow Pages" would be our only source of information. Victor had to have triple-by-pass surgery. I went to the hospital chapel with all of the children, and I prayed aloud, "Please, Lord, give us time with him." My husband had been a very strong man but now, suddenly, he had a weak heart. With this major change in our life, I continued to struggle, trying to understand what was happening. I felt so lost and so alone, being in a state so far away from all my friends and extended family members. I missed them so much, even though the children were nearby. They were happy, but I still had a void in my life that I could not fill.

Victor retired immediately after his surgery at age 59. My husband really didn't seem to mind retiring and, upon his recovery, kept himself busy in the garage. Then Tillie Scaffariello, a good friend from North Haven, asked if her son, Jim, could come and live with us in California. I was only too happy to accommodate my dear friend. So now I had my husband, my youngest child, David, and Jim—all living in our home. Yet I was still unhappy and feeling incomplete—home all day thinking, "How boring this is!" Although all of my adult children lived nearby in California, somehow I always kept feeling I did not belong there. Later in 1981, after the death of his wife, my brother, Duke, came out from Long Island, New York, to live with me for a while. Now I didn't feel quite so lonely. It was good, having another member of my family close by in the house—especially my brother Ciro (Duke) who I loved so much.

It wasn't long after that when my husband took over the cooking and shopping. He had complained that I was spending too much money on food and then decided that steaks, veggies, salads and fruits were now out of the question. Good old pasta, with a side vegetable mixed in, would be our new nightly dinner dish. I thought, "Lord, *this* has to change. I can't live like this." I was a nervous wreck. Then one day, I happened to be driving down Ventura Boulevard and noticed an ad for a class called "LIVE AND LEARN." I thought to myself, "This is a start! Why not?"

The class would be quite a positive experience for me. I attended the class every night for thirty days. Did I learn anything? Yes! Thank You, Lord! Afterward, as a result, I soon enrolled in community college classes to improve my work skills. I took business courses in computers. I learned how to type on an electric typewriter and took a course in accounting where I earned an "A!" Believe it or not, it all came to me easily. It was God's way of telling me I could do anything I put my mind to. This experience would lead me to a position as an accountant, even before I received my "Certificate of Completion." *(*LOL *Big deal!)* I went to an employment agency and was hired on the spot by an accounting firm on Ventura Boulevard. My boss was an "Angel" and I know my work pleased him. My job was great while it lasted – until my boss's wife started coming to the office and giving me orders. She made it quite apparent to me that I had no place there. So I politely quit *and* politely told her she could have her job back.

During the eight years we lived in California, my son Chuck went out on his own and worked for a boat builder, while David continued his schooling. It seemed that everything was falling into place, but the Lord had other plans for me. It was now time for a big change.

Chapter Eleven

To My Family …

Gosh, where did all the years go? I was so busy bringing you up that I never realized where the time went. How lucky can we be? Or is it how good God is to us? God will always be, with each and every one of you. In my remaining years I ask only ONE thing of you in your lives: Love God, believe and trust in Him above all things, and He will be there for you when you need Him. Many years of life have proven to me how much and what an important part the Lord and his Blessed Mother are in my life. I never mentioned it to anyone because it might have sounded like I was "off my rocker."

With love and prayers, every beautiful gift
is the Lord, telling us how much he loves us
when we believe in him.

Mom

My Breath of Life

A Letter to my Children
May 8, 1984
For You, My Children:

My children, my love for all of you has been my Breath of Life. Where did the years all go? (From 1948 to 1984—all 36 of them) I write "Breath of Life" because I *lost* my breath:

Victor: when you almost fell down the hill at Fort Hale Park, Aug. 15, 1958. God was with you.

Paul: when you almost drowned and I received the call from Griffin Hospital. God was with you.

Madelyn: when you almost drove your car off of the cliff on Christmas Eve. God was with you.

Robert: when the fish hook wrapped around your finger, (and you almost lost it). God was with you.

Chuckie: when the tip of your finger came off. God was with you.

David: when you were in your little beach chair by the pond and Robert and Madelyn were supposed to be babysitting while I went to the store. They were in the middle of the pond on the raft and you were on the shore. Somehow your chair toppled over and you were face down in the water! Thank God, Duke, our dog and saviour was there and he pulled you out! Madelyn and Robert swam to shore and they changed your clothes immediately before their mom "The Sergeant" got home.

It was a miracle! God was with you, David—and God was with *me,* too! I believe I always felt Him and my Blessed Mother's presence near.

There are numerous other "close calls." I'm sure I don't even know about some of them, but God does.

Here are a few more of the close calls when God was with you:

Victor: when you totaled the new Impala going uphill on a freeway on Postman's Highway in Connecticut and the car crash in Virginia after you went AWOL in the Navy. Also, the time you almost drowned in Italy—and I'm sure there were others.

Paul: The night you were left in the ditch on Highway 91 in the snow. Only God and you knew your fears, dangers, and what you had to do to survive in Viet Nam. Yes, God was with you or you wouldn't be here.

Madelyn: When I left the hot pack on your chest, and when your gums blew up and looked like they would never go down.

Robert: You were about the only one that I prayed for in Boston when you were at college. You looked lost and then found your way.

Chuckie: Remember the day we were in your little MG midget and it rolled over and we walked out without a scratch? Personally, that is the closest I ever came to dying. I called out, "Blessed Mother be with us now!" After this accident, I felt a miracle was happening that day and night. I sat in the middle of my bed the next morning and could not for the life of me comprehend what had happened to me.

Your father: Stricken with a heart disease but God gave him another chance.

I could go on and on. I love each and every one of you in my own special way. "A love that **never** dies."

With love,

Mom

Chapter Twelve

My "Good Life" in Las Vegas

My feelings were strong when I was 10, stronger when I was 20, stronger when I was 30—then in my 60th year, they became the strongest ever.

. . . Gloria Vanacore

We made our big move to Las Vegas, a place Victor and I had visited frequently in 1984. We also invited Robert and his family to come and live with us there. He and his wife had been in the restaurant business and thought the cost of living was more affordable in Vegas. He also liked the area, the climate, and the employment possibilities. After the large move to Las Vegas, I couldn't believe I was there myself. At first I thought, as I often did at turning points in my life, "What on earth am I doing here?" Who would ever believe we would end up in Las Vegas? I believe now that the Lord sent me to Las Vegas, because it was where I was finally meant to be.

We got lucky when we moved into Elmwood Village's model apartment just off of Maryland Parkway in the southwest part of town. We lived in the apartment for about five years while we continued to still own our home in California. I soon began thinking, "Gosh, this is fun!" In Las Vegas I could play poker and video machines anytime, although my passions were Live Poker, Texas Hold'em, and Omaha! We had played poker for twenty years with a group of friends in New Haven, so I did have a little experience! Back then it had been fun for both of us, but now we were in Las Vegas far from our friends from earlier times. This was different! Of course I needed money to play, so I decided to seek work at an employment agency. Again, I was immediately hired as a temp for a phone soliciting company. Next, I got a job at CitiBank, typing credit card accounts into their computer system. It was interesting to me.

In the beginning, it seemed like we were so lucky! Besides playing in some poker tournaments, we also played Hold'em, Omaha, Hi-Lo and Bingo—and we were winning! I said, "Gosh Vic, we could make a living out of this!" But now I believe we were being tested, or possibly tempted, with our good luck. At any rate, it was all good fun to win. We even won some of the small poker tournaments. But our luck didn't last!

Truthfully, I really did not ever have my heart in gaming completely and still felt something was missing in my life. I also strongly felt that we should make a decision to buy a house in Las Vegas rather than to go on renting an apartment. So we sold our home in California in order to find a home to purchase in Vegas. I did not want to touch any of our savings from the sale of our home, but I soon noticed that we were starting to dip into it—and still living in the apartment. Somehow it was not right, because I was working, gambling, paying rent, yet not owning my own home. I kept thinking, "There has to be something better than this." We were not going any place with this lifestyle. I told Vic, "This is *not* going to happen!" While looking for a new house I prayed, "Lord, let us pick out the right spot." We scouted from east to west in town and finally decided on a home in the northwestern part of Vegas. It was on a cul-de-sac called Coastal Breeze Court.

We both wondered, "Should we or shouldn't we buy this home? Is this where we really want to reside?" It was a small, modest home with two bedrooms—a perfect size for us. My husband, Victor, felt comfortable with it and, by this point in time, it no longer really mattered to me. For some strange reason, I didn't care to differ with him. I thought it would cause too much friction for the family. Even though our home in California had been much more comfortable, it had never felt like a *real* home to me. I felt this was going to be our last move *and* our last home together, do or die. So we sold our California home and bought our home on Coastal Breeze in Las Vegas.

So as the Lord willed it—we did just that. We found a Catholic church nearby. Up to this moment, I'd had many significant "life experiences," but the realization of my faith came fully to me only after we had moved into our home on Coastal Breeze Court. You will understand how this happened as the following chapters unfold. By 1989 my husband noticed that I was moody and complaining. I was again feeling a strange void inside of me that I could not explain. I no longer had my heart in gaming, as it was consuming our income day after day. Vic seemed to be enjoying himself, but for me it wasn't enough. I knew now that something was *really* missing in my life. Vic sensed it and just told me to get over it. He said, "Get a Life."

I thought, "What kind of life?" We gambled day and night for years and, although he was satisfied with that, I deeply yearned to find something more profound to devote my time to. By then I missed my children and friends. I also had developed a compelling urge to join the Legion of Mary at our new parish and decided to join. That decision, along with a *very* special surprise visit with a beautiful traveling "pilgrim" in my new Las Vegas home, would be the beginning of my *new* Life's Journey.

I truly believed that our family praying together would have the effect the Reverend Fulton J. Sheen mentioned so often: "The family that prays together stays together."
We prayed the Rosary together frequently.

This is a photograph of my newest Rosary. It was given to me recently as a gift. Pictured on the medal is our new, wonderful Pope Francis!

My Uplifting Story
"The Pilgrim Statue of Our Lady of Fatima"

When I look back, my Lord had a hand in every move I ever made, and I believe in my heart that during this period and in this place, Las Vegas, was where my spiritual life began. We had moved to the northwest side of Las Vegas by 1989, and the following February was the first "incident" that really began *my own* deep, spiritual understanding of what *my* life was all about. It was the following experience with the Pilgrim Statue. Oh, how I wish I had understood sooner, but who really does? I don't believe anyone does until some strange encounter or experience comes into their lives. It is strange because I realize that if we had the answers and believed in them, we would all make a complete turn-around. We would all try to think carefully about what is really important and what *isn't !!!* Should I? Or could I? Is it the right choice? Am I doing the right thing? All I can remember is that I never did or considered anything alone. I always pondered and prayed diligently. Did it make sense? Yes, to me it did. It may have seemed like a weakness to me—so be it. I always felt that I couldn't go on without going to my God and seeking his help. Oh! How pleased I am now to have done those things and to have felt the way I did!

The first Saturday we were in the house, which was devoid of furniture, I decided to attend a Mass at our new Catholic church, St. Francis de Sales. After Mass I had planned on going to the mall but felt that I needed to stay a little longer in the church. A little Mexican lady seated in the pew in front of me kept looking around with a somber expression. I asked her what was wrong. She looked at me and replied, "I don't understand. Every Saturday someone comes up to me and asks to take home the parish statue of Our Lady of Fatima, to keep it for a week, and return it the following Saturday." No one had yet asked her. She told me that they call the *Pilgrim Statue*, a "visiting statue." I said to her, "Gosh! I would love it, but we haven't furnished our home as yet."

She said, "It doesn't matter because she will fit anywhere you want to put her." So. I agreed to take the *Pilgrim Statue* home. I packed her gently in a blanket and placed her on the floor of the back seat of my car and drove home. My husband saw me coming into our driveway and said, "What on earth are you doing at home? I thought you were going to the mall." I happily replied, "I just couldn't leave my Blessed Mother in the car alone while I went shopping." I couldn't wait to bring her into our new home, never realizing what effect she would have on me during that week. I placed her on the tile step in front of our fireplace. Of course the room was empty since we did not yet have our furniture. Well that week it became my daily prayer kneeling place—a special adventure in our new home in Las Vegas. How about that!

The Friday before the day I was to return her, it was 3:00 p.m. in the afternoon when I sensed the fragrance of roses in the air. I felt such a sense of peace, like never before. I ran into the kitchen, grabbed my husband's hand, and said, "You must come and kneel before the Blessed Mary, and please tell me what you feel." He came in, looked startled, and said, "I smell flowers!" Indeed, it was the scent of roses! When I brought back the statue the following morning at 8:00 a.m., I told the little Mexican lady what had happened. She smiled and said, "Oh! I am so pleased. Not many people have that experience, but some do."

How Could I Not Believe?

Love, faith in mankind, service to others—
visiting the sick, feeding the poor.
I am all thine, My Queen,
and all that I have is thine, Sweet Mother –
All that I do is for you.

Chapter Thirteen

The Legion of Mary 1989

Compassion, Consolation, and Conversion

I have had my faith since I was a child. When my husband and I moved to Las Vegas and attended a Sunday Mass at St. Francis de Sales parish, we heard the Pastor, Monsignor Le Voy mention the Legion of Mary. The Legion of Mary is an association of Catholic laity, including men and women, who spread their faith while growing their faith for Jesus in union with Mary, His most perfect disciple. He made an appeal to the congregation for more parishioners to join. It was at that moment when I felt a compelling urge to become a member of the Legion. The following are my early notes, written during the time when I first became a member of the Legion of Mary at St. Francis de Sales Church in Las Vegas:

My First Meeting

I attended my first meeting. Monsignor Le Voy asked me why I wanted to join the Legion of Mary. I answered, "Because I love the Blessed Mother."

He smiled and said, "That is the best reason I've ever heard." That conversation marked the beginning of a new spiritual life for me! I immediately knelt down and joined the women reciting the Rosary. The candles were lit on each side of the Blessed Mother. Two fresh-cut flowers in vases were placed next to each candle. This was the protocol at all meetings. At that special moment, I finally felt like I belonged. This was it! At that moment I finally realized that God put me on this earth for a reason.

Then the meeting continued. When the secretary concluded reading the notes of the previous meeting, she looked at Monsignor and said, "I apologize. I'm so sorry. I must resign my secretarial duties. I won't be able to attend any meetings in the future. You will need to find someone to take the notes."

Monsignor looked around and said, "Would anyone like to volunteer?" No one replied. After a moment I said, "Father, years ago I held a secretarial position. I could try." Nodding his head with a sweet and gentle smile, he said, "I am *sure* you can do it. It's easy. You just have to follow a format. It's settled!" With those words, I began my crusade for the Legion of Mary, and my work as the Legion secretary.

I had a most gratifying and peaceful experience. All those years in the past, I had asked my Blessed Mother for so many favors. I had prayed and begged her to intercede for me when I felt my family life was falling apart. She was always *there* for me. Now it was my turn to serve her. So, with my Rosary in hand and the love for my Lord and His Mother, I would do whatever it took to make me one of her faithful disciples.

My Second Meeting

After my second Legion of Mary meeting, I began my duties as secretary. We had a vote and named our Praesidium, "Queen of the Apostles." The president, Mary Mac, a tall, thin, attractive woman, assigned Elizabeth Pereline and me to be partners. First, we were given a list of patients to visit at the El Jen Care Center and Retirement Home in Las Vegas. We were both new to the whole idea, so our first visitation was very strange. We had not been trained in the proper routine. All we knew was that we had to greet the patients in the correct manner. Then, if they wished, we could say a prayer with them. We felt like aliens. Some of the patients must have thought we looked like them too. Here we were all dressed up except, for the fact, that Elizabeth had a straw hat on. I wondered if I should go and get one too! I thought, "Gee, what are we going to say to these people?" They were all sleeping!

Then we saw some residents that were out of their beds, wandering the halls and having conversations with themselves. One elderly lady in a wheelchair, seemingly in possession of all her faculties, called out to me and asked, "Are you coming to my wedding?" I walked over to see her and held her hand. She said, "Oh Sister, I was waiting for you. You took too long. Where did you go?" Clearly she thought I was her sister, so I politely went along with her.

At that time, the care center was not nearly as meticulous and clean as it is today. There was a terrible stench of urine and other rancid odors in the corridor. Walking with Elizabeth, such a prim and proper lady, I had to keep one hand over my mouth.

The Next Meeting

At the next Legion of Mary meeting, everyone reported the results of their visits. I was, by this time, the acting secretary. Our president, Mary Mac, informed us that we had gone to the El Jen Care Center at the wrong time of day and decided to join us at our following visit. Walking into the Care Center with Mary was an entirely different experience. She had obviously been doing this for years, because her approach was very natural. Most important was that she had a beautiful demeanor with the patients. I continue to hope, as the time goes by, that my return visits will give me the same self-assurance that she had. I was pleased with the patients I visited, particularly Nino—known to be the "Grouch" who was very friendly with us. Another resident named Irene, though a loner, was also cordial and glad to pray with us.

The Following Week

The following week I read the minutes from the previous week and recorded the work of the members such as: evangelization, feeding the poor, visiting the sick, and administering the Eucharist. We chose Wednesdays to become our visiting days, unless there was a change in plans. The members also discussed the upcoming "March for Life," which was to take place the following month.

Another *"Yes"* to Our Lady!

About two years later Mary Mac had to leave the Legion of Mary, because her husband had become ill and needed her care at home. While we were attending the "Acies"—a meeting held to renew Legionary vows held at Holy Family Church, Mary confronted me in front of a large statue of Our Lady. She told me about her husband's illness and said, "Monsignor suggested that I ask you to take over the presidency."

I replied, "Who, me? I don't think I could do it." She said, "Monsignor had his reasons as to why he chose you." I felt that Mary was putting me in an awkward situation. I said, "You do such a good job as our president. How could I ever fill your shoes?"

Mary glanced up at the statue of Our Blessed Mother and looked down at me saying, "Are you going to *refuse* Our Lady?"

Of course I would not refuse Our Blessed Mother … and, of course, I said "Yes" to Mary! I would soon begin my duties as the new president of the Legion of Mary.

Some people would call the Legion of Mary a cult, but quite to the contrary, by no means is it anything like a cult. Joining the Legion, a small group of women at the time, was my first encounter with true closeness to Our God and to my Blessed Mother. The mission of the Legion of Mary begins with three words: compassion, consolation, and conversion. There are rules and regulations, as I'm sure there are in most clubs and organizations we join, but our rules were not easy.

At the time I found the required two hours of weekly volunteering strenuous. The visits could have been anywhere: care centers, rehabilitation homes, door-to-door evangelizing, visiting the sick, or feeding the poor. Later in that same year, I would also became a Eucharistic Minister. Our parish in Las Vegas, a city with many urban problems and temptations, was loaded with opportunities for volunteer service and benevolence. Gosh! Where else on earth could I find all of this?

My Friend Anthony

While visiting the El Jen Care Center in 1990, a gentleman named Anthony happened to be one of the patients. The third time I visited him there, he meekly said, "Gloria, I would like to do the work just the way you're doing it." He was referring to my Legion of Mary service of visiting and comforting the sick. "Is there a chance for me? I am not the man I used to be," he added. I told Anthony to speak to the pastor of our church, Monsignor Le Voy. I added, "We would love to have you help us in our Legion of Mary. This town is growing and we would love to extend the Legion to other churches here." Here was a man who in his earlier years had been a heavy drinker, smoker, married and divorced, quite a "ladies man," and only the Lord knows what else!

Anthony's rapid transformation was just unbelievable! Almost immediately he became a Eucharistic Minister and did his service at El Jen. He would soon also need a partner to begin service with the Legion Of Mary. We always did our service in pairs. He asked me if I would join him and also suggested that I become a Eucharistic Minister too. I replied instantly, "Not *me*! I don't feel worthy enough. Who am I? I can't even find *myself*. Are you for real?" Anthony gave me a sweet, soft smile and said, "If I can do it, why can't you? You seem to catch the attention of the patients."

I gave his idea careful thought and consideration and decided, "Gosh, if I can make people happy and see a sign of peace on their faces by being a Eucharistic Minister, why not?" A year later in 1991, I also became a Eucharistic Minister. Now due to the intolerable stench still at the care center in those days, I had to decide if I would become Anthony's partner as a Eucharistic Minister at that location. Anthony had chosen me. He had become my friend. I decided to say "Yes" to Anthony, not realizing that I was really saying "Yes" to GOD! By this time Anthony had been released from the Care Center and was living in a trailer. We would always go together. We would talk about our private lives and discuss things that had happened to us when we were children, and some of the stupid choices we had made along the way.

On our weekly visits, we would recite the Rosary and explain the mysteries of the Life of Christ. Sometimes Anthony would lose his breath and try to use his breathing apparatus. He had never completely recovered from emphysema. Then as weeks went by, he would sometimes leave during our services and ask me to take over. I was timid at first, but with My Blessed Lady's help and knowing how much it meant to Anthony, I had the fortitude to go on. I kept saying to myself, "I must at least *try*!" Anthony used to encourage me and say, "Gloria—the patients are half asleep and can't even hear you!"

One Wednesday, which would be the last of Anthony's visits with me for our Rosary Service, he had to leave abruptly. He looked directly at me and said, "Gloria, I can't go on! Take over. I am tired and want to get home." Of course I did as he asked, but I thought, "He'd better get well. He started all of this and originally I was supposed to only be supporting him."

Anthony died that very evening. It was on exactly the same evening that my family and loved ones would have *three accidents in one day*, which you will read about in a moment. I didn't find out about his death right away. The following Tuesday, I went in to our next Legion of Mary meeting and found out, sadly, that Anthony had passed away. I prayed secretly to My Lord that day and said, "Lord, I will never say 'No,' if I can do something for You when it comes to service for others. I know You are there. I know You are real. And I do know You are in my heart and will be pleased!"

Faith · Love · Trust

Our Legion of Mary altar, carefully arranged with candles and flowers Our Blessed Mother is so beautiful---the mother of Our Savior, Jesus.

Legion of Mary members at the Rosary Session on Ash Wednesday at the El Jen Care Center: (left to right) Laura, Marlene, Liz, and Gloria

Love with Trust and Faith in God.

Three Accidents—All in One Day

The day before these accidents I was in a dilemma. As a member of the Legion of Mary, my duty was to go to the El Jen Care Center, say the Rosary, and pray with the sick and lonely every Wednesday. Saying the Rosary was easy—like talking to God. On February 13, 1991, I came home from one of my weekly visits *at* El Jen depressed. I had been looking into the eyes of the patients, feeling their troubled and somewhat confused minds. I thought to myself, "There is something *better* for me to do. How could I even handle this?" My husband, Victor, realized how sad these times made me, and he didn't think it was a good idea to continue my activities with the Legion of Mary if it was going to make me feel that way.

About one hour after I arrived home, my phone rang. It was an emergency call from the Las Vegas Medical Center. They said to me, "Your son Arthur Vanacore, was in an accident. His car ended up in a ravine in Desert Mountain. He was picked up by an Angel Flight and right now he is in the emergency room." I realized they were talking about my second youngest son, Chuck, and my heart dropped. Immediately my husband, Victor, and I rushed to the hospital. While driving I kept praying and asking the Lord to spare Chuck's life. "Another accident?" I thought to myself, "Oh God, not *again!* Lord, how many times in my lifetime are You going to give me back my children? I have come to You, time and time again—and there You are."

I even began bargaining with the Lord, telling Him that I would start visiting the El Jen Convalescent Home every weekend and never give it up for the rest of my life. Right before we arrived at the hospital I said, "Please Lord, I would do anything! Just let my son come out of this dreadful accident."

When we arrived the doctors told us that it was, in fact, a miracle that Chuck was going to be released to go home with us! He had been badly burned with abrasions all over his body, so they sent prescriptions home with him. The extent of his injuries meant that he was to be kept on the medications and would need to be assisted with a cane for about a month. My heart was pounding! Right then and there I thanked my Heavenly Lord and thought, "How could I *not* go out and do a special deed at El Jen Convalescent Home and comfort those who were less fortunate than I was?"

How Could I Not Believe In Your Goodness, Lord

On our way home as Chuck and his fiancé, Cari, followed us in a separate car, I turned to my husband, hesitated, and then asked him, "Victor, why are we taking the freeway? I don't think it's a good idea."

He replied stubbornly, "Chuck and Cari are behind us. I can't change the route now."

Well, lo and behold! After driving two miles there appeared to be a figure in the middle of the road. It was a man whose car was parked nearby, standing at the side of the road. His arms were out-stretched, and he looked as if he was in need of help. Chuck and Cari were now driving two cars behind us. We stopped abruptly, and the car immediately behind us hit our rear bumper! We were startled by the impact!

The man began shouting that someone had suffered a heart attack and needed help. Victor jumped out in order to open the back door and get his cap. As I also jumped out of the car, I noticed a blue truck speeding in our direction! I said to myself, "Oh Lord, not now!" I gave a loud command, "Vic! Jump in the car! You are going to get killed!" At that time Vic was very agile, and he jumped in the car without hesitation. The truth is, I have *never* experienced anything as frightening as that as long as I have lived.

The blue truck caused a *third* accident. It was swaying down towards our lane, which was the safe lane. As the truck came by us, it swiped our rear car door off! Luckily, Vic had already jumped back into our car.

The next morning I sat on the end of my bed thinking, trying to make sense of it all. It was so incomprehensible. The driver had been drinking and was arrested for drunk driving, but everything seemed so unreal, frightening, and mysterious. Is this trying to tell me something? I realized the promise that I had made to God – and earlier to my friend, Anthony – thus, the reason for taking the Legion of Mary's Legionary Promise *"Love with trust and faith in God."* There is no answer as to why we were put on this earth. Everyone is different. No matter what path we choose on this earth, I believe it is not really for ourselves.

It is all about the choices we make and the attitude we take. I believe we all have a purpose.

My service with the Legion of Mary went on for a number of years. Even though as a child, I did have a sense of belonging to Our God and although I have always tried to love and please others, I had never really felt I was worthy to receive such a gift—that divine gift of "Faith, Love, and Trust." I chose Laura to be my partner along with Elizabeth (Shean), and Mary. As time went on, El Jen became my Life's Journey with a love and service for My God which I cannot totally explain. My favorite duties are visiting the sick, praying with the patients, and feeding the poor – and I am still ministering the Eucharist to this day

How Could I Not Believe This To Be True?

The Vanacore family at David Vanacore's wedding in 1990, from left to right: Paul, David, Madelyn, Victor Sr., Gloria, Victor Jr., Robert, and Chuck.

A Letter Written to My Children

May 12, 1990 - 1991

I must admit, you are the fruits of my labor. Maybe in the years I didn't really stress the real meaning of Life and Success, but I do know that I did stress kindness, humility, and love for God and one another. I know and feel in my heart that you are still that way, as you can't rub off something that has been instilled in you, and yet life has a strange way of moving you in directions where I have no control.

Heaven knows—if I could put you all in a glass bottle and surround you with protection from all heartaches, anxieties, dangers, and evils, it would be so simple, but the Lord doesn't work that way. It is what is meant to be, but with your Trust, Faith, and Love for Him and His Blessed Mother, He will keep you in His care.

So that glass bottle to me is a symbol of His Church. Therefore, the biggest gift on this earth you can give me is to return to His House of Love with Devotion to His Beautiful Mass and the Holy Eucharist (Jesus). I said the gift is to me, but this is a gift *to you* from the Lord and me. "Live in Me and let Me live in you," says the Lord. You are all examples and role models to your children and to the people around you. Love one another as I have loved you from the day God gave you to me.

Now and Forever,
Mom

Love is patient ... Love is kind ...

It always protects, always trusts

Always hopes, always perseveres.

Love never fails

St. Paul Corinthians 13:4

Chapter Fourteen
My Eucharistic Mission

On the morning I was to become a Eucharistic Minister, I awoke from a deep sleep. I could have sworn that I saw a ghost-like figure of the Blessed Mother emerging out of the bare wall, then gracefully flowing across the foot of my bed. I could feel her warmth. I cried in a loud voice and asked her to wait, but she slowly faded away. I was so excited and ran into my husband's room, where he was sleeping. (Like so many couples, after many years we had decided to have separate bedrooms.) I shook him and said, "Vic, you are not going to believe me! I saw the Blessed Mother! You wouldn't believe it." He answered, "Gloria, I believe you!" Well, I'm glad he did, because no one else would have.

Over time I have been asked by others, "What does she look like?" I always say, "I can't explain it, but she is beautiful!" Of course, back then it all didn't make any sense to me. I simply couldn't believe that she would appear to me *personally* although this was the same day I was assigned to become a Eucharistic Minister. It wasn't until later that I actually connected these two events. As a Minister, I was going to bring Communion to serve at convalescent homes and make a visit to the hospital now and then.

Me? Of all the people on earth? Who am I? I am still

trying to figure it out, even today. All I do is keep saying to myself "Oh! I love You so much, Lord. My joy is overflowing with the love I have for You and My Lady. You, My Lord, have always been there for me when I needed You the most." After that day as my life as a Eucharistic Minister began, my Sundays became easier. It was no longer such a chore for me. The words came to me naturally, and I became very comfortable with what I was doing.

"Lady Marion"

Marion Denver came into my life in 1992, shortly after Anthony passed away. She was a true "lady," perfect in every way. She had an especially sweet demeanor, a wonderful smile, and perpetual patience—as well as gentleness, a good sense of humor, and the perfect love for *Our Lady of Fatima.* Our two years of friendship went by as if it were a lifetime, though it seemed like our time together was never long enough. Our love and friendship became stronger than anything I have ever felt for someone during my lifetime. I have frequently asked myself, "How could I ever have met such a beautiful soul?" Well, this is how it happened.

One morning the phone rang and I answered with my usual "Hello." Marion replied very sweetly, "You don't know me, but I just read the church bulletin. Your name, telephone number, and offer of kindness was like a gift from God. I could use a ride now and then to Church, and I would so like to attend the one o'clock Mass on Sundays.

I love that Mass and also just love hearing Joe Farina and his family play the music for it. I do not expect it every Sunday but, if you do attend it, I would love a ride." I wrote Marion's phone number down, called her later, and told her that I would give her a ride the following Sunday. Gosh, she sounded so happy, responding to my offer in her sweet, demure voice. She had been reluctant to phone me, because she didn't want to be a burden on anyone but, in fact, this was the beginning of a beautiful friendship.

Little did I know that I had just met a lady named Marion whom I would never, ever, forget! While talking to her on the phone, I felt that I already knew her, as I assured her that I would pick her up in front of the club house of her apartment complex. She said very sweetly, "You can't miss me, Gloria. You don't know what I look like, but you will see an old lady with a cane in front of our club house. You will recognize me immediately."

That Sunday she waited for me, dressed in a pretty blue suit with a white, lace-collar blouse, and not a hair was out of place. Marion had a smile that I'd never forget. She took my hand, looked at me, and gave me a loving thank you. I helped her into the car and we were on our way to Mass. We sat together in the third pew. She did not want to miss anything. I would end up taking her to Sunday Mass regularly. Later we began to go shopping on Wednesdays, now and then, together and occasionally to the bank on Fridays. Marion also loved playing the slot machines. Her face would even light up and turn red. Her eyes were glued on the red, white, and blue sevens with a look of hope!

I did not know at first that *Lady* Marion was the mother of Bob Denver, a star in the television series, *Gilligan's Island.* One day she casually mentioned that she had to go to the mailbox and send some of his fan mail responses. She would also often mention her love for her daughter, Helen, and her husband, Artie. She told me how devoted they all were to one another. Many nights we would chat on the phone and laugh at all of our experiences!

Our last encounter was the evening before she passed away. It was our final telephone conversation. I had called her earlier in the week to ask what time she would be ready for me to pick her up to go shopping on Friday. She sweetly replied, "I will be ready any time you want to pick me up." On Friday morning I called her early and did not get an answer. It was not like Marion, and it seemed rather strange, as she would always be so prompt in answering her phone. I felt something was wrong. I asked Vic to come with me, but he said that he was tired. So I rushed over alone. When I arrived at the rear of Marion's apartment, I knocked on her door. There was no reply, but I could hear the television. So I kept knocking on her door and shouting, "Marion!" Then I decided to go around to the front of her apartment. Since her apartment was on the first floor, I was able to squeeze between the bushes and peer through her window. Lo and behold, *there she was* on the floor—with her head between the legs of her coffee table!

I panicked like a crazy woman! I ran to the apartment supervisor's office, and he was out to lunch, but his assistant was there. I told him that I had to get in to Marion's apartment immediately! He sat there like a moron and said he didn't have a key. I shouted, "Well, *break* the door down! My friend is in trouble!" He did just that, and I rushed in and got down on the floor. Marion was still breathing! I told her I would call 911 and rushed into the kitchen to make the phone call. There I found a beautiful card and a gift on the table—meant for me. My birthday had passed just a few days before.

I also called her son Bob and met him at the hospital. Sadly, I could not speak with Marion anymore. She went into a coma and died four days later in Hospice. I just wished, with all my heart, that I could have told her how much I loved her for coming into my life. She had meant so much to me. I wanted to be able to express that to her, but I never got the opportunity. I thank My Lord for bringing "Lady Marion" into my life. Today her son's episodes on *Gilligan's Island* are still being played on television.

"Lady Marion" and the Angel Tree

A few weeks later at Christmas time 1994 I would have a strange encounter at our parish. My church, St. Francis de Sales, used to create an "Angel Tree" for the El Jen Care Center patients. Parishioners would volunteer to each purchase a Christmas gift that would be suitable for a patient. Then after we brought the gifts into our Legion of Mary home to be sorted out, the Legion members would deliver them. On that day we placed all of the gifts in a station wagon, but for some strange reason one poinsettia plant was left behind in the corner of the Legion room. With a sad look at the plant, one of the members said, "Gosh! One lonely gift is left." Since I lived closest to the El Jen Care Center, I told her that I would deliver the plant. It had a tag on it that said, "For Claire Johnson."

When I arrived at the Center, I walked up to the registration desk and asked the nurse for Claire Johnson's room number. She replied, "She died this week." I felt so dismayed, standing there with the poinsettia and said, "Now what?" The nurse replied, suggesting, "We have a woman down the hall, Marion Stellarini, that may like to have it. She has terminal cancer and is in Hospice Care. It may cheer her up."

I walked down the hall, gave a knock on her door, and walked in. Upon seeing the poinsettia, Marion smiled and said, "Oh my! It is so nice of you." I was only too happy to brighten up this patient's room. When I set the plant on her window sill, I noticed Christmas cards all over the floor. Apparently the air from the heating unit was blowing her cards off of the sill. I asked Marion if she minded that I pick the cards up and place them all back up on the window sill. "Oh! I would appreciate that, Dear!" she responded. She was so pleased! As I was finishing, I suddenly noticed one more Christmas card on the floor under her bed. I knelt down and got it. When I picked the card up, in order to place it with the others, I saw right on the front—a picture of the Blessed Mother.

I couldn't help but read the greeting. On one side of the

card it read, *Dear Marion and Artie.* I thought to myself, "My very dear friend Marion Denver's husband was also named *Artie!*" Then, on the other side of the card, it read, *from your dear friend, Gloria.* Gloria! *Gloria was my name!* Such a chill came over me. I just couldn't believe what I was seeing! This woman named *Marion* had a husband named Artie and a *dear friend named Gloria*! It was as if I were receiving a message from "Lady Marion" from beyond—a moment of divine intervention! I was a little frightened at first, "Was this something that had to happen? Was it a message? Is there any explanation for this? Was it a coincidence?" No! It was a message from My Lord! My friend, Marion Denver, *knew* how much I loved her after all! Even though I never got a chance to tell her!

How Could I Not Believe?

The following day my husband did me a favor. He played Santa Claus at the Care Center for our Angel Tree Christmas Party, giving out gifts to the patients. Heaven only knows, Vic did not have the patience or stamina to stay in a warm Santa Claus suit for an hour and a half! While he was handing out the gifts I noticed Marion Stellarini, the woman I had brought the poinsettia to the day before, in her wheel chair among the patients. She was as white as a sheet! She was still trying very hard to enjoy the Christmas party. Earlier the Legion had asked patients to specify a particular gift that they would like to receive. I handed Marion the gift with her name on it and noticed that she was finding it difficult to open. I asked if I could help her with it and she answered, "Please do."

Inside was a beautiful, blue sweater—the gift she had requested! On a card attached to her gift was written "From a St. Francis de Sales parishioner, Helen." Marion had only one daughter who was *also* named Helen! Could you say, "It was meant to be?" … that is one of my favorite expressions. Or could you simply call what happened a strange coincidence? How *strange* is that? Mysterious? Yes! *The Lord works in mysterious ways!* So, my Lady Marion, it was a wonderful two years with you. The Lord sent you to me. Or me to you. Who knows? Do you? I do—*Now!*

Slain in the Spirit
My Encounter with Jesus

It was a day when some of the ladies of the Legion of Mary decided to go to a Healing Mass with Father Rookie presiding. Healing Services are rare today. I had attended a few of them before, and I was *so* intent on going to this Mass. I thought to myself, "This time I am sure I am going to feel the healing power of My Jesus!" During the service, people wishing to be healed would usually stand up, walk to the altar, and form a line on each side. Then Father Rookie would walk along the line, blessing each person by raising his hand over their heads. There were people designated as "catchers," positioned behind the line ready to catch people as they would waiver back and forth. Then they would set them down on their backs very gently. In the Catholic faith the practice of a person falling back like this is referred to as being *Slain in the Spirit.*

After witnessing Father's healing service, I looked around and thought, "What is *wrong* with me? Why am I not falling backwards fainting or crying? I love You so much my dear Lord and I want to *feel Your presence*! I want You to know I *believe* in You." It was upsetting to me. I was even envious of the others. I felt, "Gosh, Jesus got to them but *why not to me*?" Later that evening I thought to myself, "I don't believe I will go to any more of these Healing Masses." I went to bed really tired that evening and put it all in the back of my mind. I had decided to accept it, "Oh well, it is not meant to be."

Then while I slept—lo and behold! The *beautiful* face of Jesus came to me as clearly as day! Our Lord looked straight at me—with his right arm outstretched, hand facing upwards, and with his index finger gracefully pointing straight into my heart. It woke me up! I felt a strong pain in my heart that reminded me of the heartburn I often used to experience when I was raising my children. Then I went back to sleep and when I awoke the next morning I forgot about it.

I went to Mass, for some reason, that day. I did not, at that time, attend daily Mass on a regular basis, but I had a strong desire to go. A nun I had seen the night before who had been *Slain in the Spirit*, was standing in front of the church. She was looking around and seemed to be in a quandary. She stopped to ask me as I walked by, if I knew the location of a convent in Boulder City, Nevada. I told her that although I didn't know the exact location, it was definitely somewhere in Boulder City since I had visited that convent before. I added that I had recognized her from the night before during the Healing Mass, peacefully laying on the floor after all the others had departed. I shared with the nun that nothing like that ever happened to me during a Healing Mass and that I was never going back to another one like that again.

The nun asked me what my name was. I said, "Gloria."

She replied, "You will see Him or feel His Presence when you *least* expect Him."

I said, "Oh, thank you, Sister," and I never gave it another thought after that. I was surprised when the next day, Anne Tisdale, one of our Legion of Mary members, called me and told me she had experienced a healing at the Mass. For years Anne had been a heavy smoker—up until that very morning! She said she did not go looking for her cigarettes that day. That marked the end of her smoking addiction. She had tried for many years to stop. *Thank you, Lord!* Anne is now 92 years of age and as beautiful as ever— writing her notes of faith, hoping that she can write her memoirs.

Anne and my son Chuck have been together with me at The Healing Mass. Chuck was amazed. I felt my legs trembling but I did not fall. I was behind him in line. I saw him swaying and thought, "God, he may "fall in the spirit" too, but instead he held his ground. You will be reading more about some of Chuck's spiritual experiences later in this book.

Chapter Fifteen

My Prison Ministry

In 1992 a nun came to one of our Legion of Mary meetings to speak about the prison ministry. She introduced herself as Sister Stephanie then said, "I have a *special* task for you members. I am hoping with all my heart that there is someone here who will take it on, since I will no longer be able to stay here in Las Vegas. It will be prison ministry work on every Thursday and Saturday." I quickly became intrigued because it sounded so interesting and challenging. Gosh! Prison! This would mean I could help inmates who had taken the wrong path or made poor choices and needed help. As Sister Stephanie sat right among us in our group, she gave us a pleasing smile. My heart leaped with joy! I prayed, "Lord, do You think I could do this?" By the heavens of My God and my love and trust in Him, I thought, "I am going to give it a try!"

Oh! Don't get me wrong. I did love the patients at El

Jen and always felt they were very close to the Lord. Some were elderly or sick, and some were in Hospice ready to meet their Maker—but *prison!* What better way could I serve my Lord than to go to the inmates who really needed prayers and spiritual guidance. I even thought it would be my "high"—an experience and feeling I would remember forever! I never dreamed in a million years that I was going to feel so much adrenaline rushing through my blood stream when I went to begin that first day of my prison ministry. And this "rush" continued on many of the following Thursdays and Saturdays while I was there.

On the first Saturday I was a nervous wreck, so I attended Mass beforehand at Saint Joan of Arc Church. Fortunately the Church was right across the street from the Clark County Detention Center where I was assigned to serve my prison ministry. After Mass I walked across the street and began this new journey. Naturally the Prison Ministers had to follow the same rules as all of the other visitors who entered the jail. We were allowed to bring in Bibles, Rosary Beads, and appropriate literature for our ministry, but on every visit the contents of our bags were always scanned before entering the building. I used to call the jail a dungeon because it was always so cold.

Truthfully, I never felt as good as I did in the presence of all of those lost souls, both young and old. I could now do something more for Our Lord Jesus Christ! I call the prisoners "lost souls" because I believe that though they made their choices, they never realized at the time the consequences they would face by being sent to prison.

Being in prison meant that they would neither see their families nor know the outcome of their sentences. I always thought to myself, "These *poor* kids! Where did they go wrong?" I looked at their faces during our deep prayers and meditation. They were saddened. I knew they missed their family members. Our prayer meetings and talks were wonderful. Many of them gave their input and spoke freely about their families and home lives.

As the weeks turned into months and years, ministering to the prisoners came with ease and with a great *love* for those who were so much less fortunate than I was. There were some inmates who wanted to know more about the Christian faith. When our services were announced over the PA system, the announcer would say that all denominations were welcome and that all inmates were invited, but everyone knew that it would be a Catholic religious service. On some days they would flock in—sometimes they would even number over a hundred in the jail's gymnasium. At times we had to stop counting those who attended!

For a while we also did services on Thursdays at the Mojave Jail on Eastern Avenue in Las Vegas. When I first visited the Mojave Jail, the services combined men and women inmates. It was trying at times. We soon noticed that the women were not exactly paying full attention to our message. They seemed to be more interested in the men. Naturally! So we asked the attending guard if we could schedule services for men and women on alternate weeks. I must admit I felt good actually knowing that I was reaching the hearts of many whom I met along the way. Doing the ministry I felt as if I "belonged" there. Deep in my heart I felt I could really help them and that my life finally had *a meaning!*

My co-partner was Carol Desmond, a dear friend. We all had to do our service in pairs and we were free to choose partners. Our ministry leader would match up contrasting co-workers, because we all had different views and individual experiences. I chose Carol because as an infant she was dropped on a doorstep in a basket at a convent. A note had been placed in the basket that read, "Just give her Jewish parents." So Carol had never known her biological parents, was adopted by a Jewish family, and left the convent when she was 15 years old. When I started ministering with her, I was so nervous and apprehensive because I didn't know how or where to begin.

I could not have asked for a better partner. Carol began the service by introducing us and then spoke to the prisoners as if she were one of them. She had been a runaway as a child. Since they paid close attention to her every word, I was so pleased. Then I would begin the religious service by reading the *Good News* Bible. I also led short prayers, followed by a question and answer period. We expressed ourselves with the word of God: "The Way, the Truth and the Light." We had to complete the whole service in one hour and concluded with the *Lord's Prayer.* Then we would ring a bell to summon the section "G" security guard who would walk in and say, "Time is up." The prisoners always pleaded for more time.

Even today I still keep thinking, "What is wrong with this picture, Lord? Why does it have to be this way? It just isn't fair. Yes, they did make their choices, but *Why?* Yes, they put themselves in those situations, but *Why?*" Oh, how I wish I had the answers! Yet I am not on this earth to judge, either—so I am back to square one.

Letters from Prison

While ministering at the Clark County Detention Center, I received letters from some of the inmates. They were not allowed to know our addresses, phone numbers, or even our last names, so they would send letters to our church addressed "St. Francis de Sales, Legion of Mary, Las Vegas." Some of them poured their hearts out to me as you will see on the following pages …

From Luthia: "With God—I Win …"

One very special woman named Luthia wrote to me telling me how sorry she was for her offense, then how grateful she was to *believe* and have a second chance thanks to her finding a spiritual side of life. Well, Luthia was finally home after doing time. She says she never did have a spirit to begin with. If she had she would not have looked for drugs and be in a position of prostitution (the easy way out). But for a helping hand from God, she was able to see a new direction in her life as she expressed in her letters to me during and after she left prison.

December 24, 1999
Praise God!
Dear Gloria and family,

I thank God for a beautiful friend like you. Upon receiving your card, I'm in prayer that all is well and the holidays are in a cheerful spirit for you and your loved ones. The card you sent me was beautiful. It did bring tears to my eyes to read what you wrote to me. I know in my heart that you're a very special God-Sent person. He placed you in my life and was an instrument to turn me around—so glad I did. I am wondering what took me so long to see the right way to go. Believe me, Satan is powerful. He puts blinders on everyone so that they are easily led down the wrong path. It's up to us to deny him control over our lives.

I'm truly a blessed woman, a Child of God. These are special times for us and each day is a reminder to rejoice over the many wonderful gifts God has given us and seek ways to show people that we love and appreciate them for being who they are and not for what they can do for us. I see so much misery here, Gloria. A lot of the women love the Lord but Satan has his hand in the pie, too. They are really out of touch with the real cause for celebrations, Christ coming and the preparation to receive Him. I seek the Lord's forgiveness of my sins daily, because I want to be in the Book of Life and live with Him forever in glory.

There are so many ways to celebrate God's gifts of our lives and our relationships and of Himself.

When we rejoice in his name through our willingness to share, to love one another, and to grow spiritually—I know when I'm doing it right. Satan does his thing to try to turn me around but I refuse to go back the wrong way. Temptation is one of his vices used against you, instead of for you. Am I correct? With God I win, with Satan I lose. It's up to me and all believers and unbelievers which one path we decide to choose—just something that came to mind.

Gloria, God is so good to me daily. I thank Him for all my many blessings, both large and small. I'm working hard. I've been promoted to Senior Hall Porter. I'm in charge. (Smile) My duties grow each day, but I am working for the Lord and they are easier to get through. I read where it says, "In all things done in the name of Jesus, you will grow spiritually and become prosperous." Maybe not worded this way, but some effort, and it gets me on my way when I start to slip. I have a paying job now. Praise the Lord, and the boss actually depends on me and trusts my judgment about things to be done. I'm trusted! Praise the Lord. How many times is another life possible in which I wanted to be trusted? But Satan wouldn't have it. All I can say is that God knows I am trying to keep on the right path and that He's making the way possible. The prison isn't the worst place to be. Death could have been the result of my past.

I am thankful that He chose to spare me. I've heard about so many that I know that are now gone, and I'm pleased with the chance to change my life spiritually. Am I making sense? I can't toot my horn enough about God and what he does so well: The giver of Life, Health and Wealth, all in one breath. Amen to that! Well, I do hope your holidays are as cheerful as I hope mine will be. Considering the circumstances—as long as I have a prayer to offer up I'm pleased, because I know He hears and responds in His time.

Love to all and God bless and keep you well and in His good grace.

Love, Luthia
A Sister in Christ

from Luthia
"Jesus—there is no Sweeter Name"

April 6, 2000

Dear Gloria,

Hope all is well and you and your family are well and that prosperity is in abundance. As for myself, I'm happy and believe that through God's tender mercy, all is the way it should be. My family and I are back together, spiritually. I thought I had lost them months ago when I first came to prison, but I'm in contact and have regular responses, and it's all because I chose to go to God with things I thought were impossible. I had asked many times, "Where is God when it hurts?" Now I know; right by my side. All I had to do was just listen to Him and let Him show me the way. All I can do is depend on Him and let His love shine through.

One of the Sisters here spoke to me today, and it was a good feeling to know that my grace shows. She said that I had a glow and didn't need to wear makeup. I don't, of course, because my joy is written all over me. I have vitality that I didn't know was there. Praise the Lord Jesus for His tender mercy and his Greatness for saving me. I love the name Jesus. There is no sweeter name I know, my favorite song as well as saying, because He loves us from a world of destruction.

They all complain but actually prison is a place to go to be saved, if your attention is unattainable on the outside. Our God knows you get no other choice but to listen, locked up. But even on the streets you can be locked up within yourself and not know the Lord, because each of us are caught up with friends or sins of the flesh and overlook what is so important to maintain a wholesome life. We overlook our Savior until some trouble strikes and then, and only then, do we call the Name of the Lord. Gloria, I have lost so many of the people I called "friend" on the street. Yes, to death. And I often wonder if they had enough time to prepare for the Lord and receive His blessing of eternal life; a gift which He gives so freely. Receiving letters from you are so very comforting, and I'm so thankful to have a friend like you in my life. God only knows, if it hadn't been for you coming into the jail, I would have missed my chance to find what I was seeking and didn't have a clue that spiritual food is what was so vital for my existence. I thank you and will always treasure your friendship.

God bless and keep you safe. Keep me in your prayers and know that wherever I am, in or out, I'll be in touch. I'm going to the board again in August or September and will possibly be out between October and December. I'll make it this time. I didn't have enough yard time (two months), when I went in September, but I didn't fall by the wayside. It only made me more determined to do what was right and get my life in order. I've got the right Man on my side and through Him all things are possible.

On March 25th we walked for the Cancer Society and we received tee shirts for our participation. Quite a few people made pledges from here so it's a starting point, and Praise God, it's in the right direction, doing for others instead of being selfish as we often are. Write soon, as I'll be praying that all is well and that everyone is in a happy mood. Tell everyone "Hello."

Love,
Luthia in Christ

A second letter written from Luthia on the same day:
April 6, 2000
Dear Gloria,

Praise the Lord and His goodness. I'm thrilled to hear from you. I don't know how you do it, but then again, Yes, I do! I'm still growing in my spiritual walk. There is no turning back. I've come to face the reason that I've not been faithful in my letters. I've been very busy, and they keep me hopping here. Can you believe it?—an inmate that they depend on. And I do get the job done—and important responsibilities too! Some things I can take to the street as back up for employment, plus I am still in school at night. I keep a full schedule; no time for the adversity to tempt me, (smile). God has plans for my life and this is apparent. What those are I'm unsure of at the time but it can only get better. As we know our Lord Jesus is a very subtle person. The plans He makes are the kind you can't get out of or put off. And besides that, I couldn't depend on anyone else to see me through the trials or handle the daily fears of not being able to handle life's situations.

I'm so glad to be in prison. I feel like I'm nuts for saying it, but it's true. If I had not come here, I would have been dead or in a way that no help or hope would be possible. He, "The Lord," sent me here to save me from all harm and danger, show me my worth and that I too am His, and that He loves me unconditionally. I see so many come and go—ones who say they have changed their lives but a month goes by and they're back. I pray for strength to face life on the outside and in here, and once I'm out I'll not return here. I've been here nine months now, and it's the best time I've spent anywhere. No matter what I do, I thank the Lord for his many blessings that he grants me every day. I have about six more months and I'll be out, and believe me, you can rest assured that I'll find a way and a place of worship to keep in touch with my salvation, which means so much to me.

Life is too precious to not live it with Jesus and no matter what anyone says, believe me, Jesus, our blessed Savior, makes a way out of no way. I'm a firm believer that all my needs are placed within my grasp. All I've got to do is trust Him, and I do.

Gloria, I thank God every day for placing you in my life. You just don't know what an inspiration that you and Willie are to me. Give my love and "Hellos" to everyone and let each one know that they are blessed to be in the arms of the Almighty. Jesus loves us so much that the pain and the suffering is made easy when we turn our lives around. I love you.

Your friend in Christ,
Luthia

Joshua's Letter

My grandson Joshua's letter to me, written from prison:

From Joshua
April 15, 2014

Noni !
Hey—how's everything? I received your letters, as well as the money for my birthday and I just wanted to thank you so much! The money is going to my "coming home" outfit —and you know that I'm very excited for that! I also just wanted to thank you for all your love and support over

the past 8 1/2 years. Your words and your letters found me at times when I needed them the most, and gave me the strength and the courage that I needed to persevere through the many, many obstacles placed in my way. There are no words I can find to describe my appreciation for having you and our caring family with me. As the time comes to a close, my eyes are fully open and able to see the righteousness of God and the strength that you can gain from faith. I've learned a great many things, but what I take away from this the most is that life is truly about *faith and family*. *That* is true wealth, true happiness and true love. I've seen and been through the *worst,* but I've learned to humble myself with the knowing that, no matter what happens or how bad it gets ... I truly have my faith and my family. Thank you so much for helping me to realize that because it will forever be with me. With all that being said, I love you so much and can't wait to see you! Take care and much love always!

Joshua

PRAYER OF CONSECRATION

Almighty Father, we consecrate ourselves and our home to the Sacred Heart of Jesus, who loves us with a tender and everlasting love.

May we return this love to Him in the way we treat, respect, and love each other.

We pledge to live our lives together in the ways of Christ Jesus.

We welcome Jesus as a living member of our family. We invite Him to be the Heart of our family.

We accept Mary as our heavenly Mother. We implore her protection and help in our daily lives.

May our love go beyond our home into the world, so that we may do our part to build up Your kingdom, to feed the hungry, to help the poor, and to lead all souls to Your Sacred Heart.

Amen.

This is the devotional " A Family Blessing: Prayer of Consecration". I have passed this pamphlet out to so many of my family, friends and fellow parish members. It was created by the Priests of the Sacred Heart, Sacred Heart Monastery, PO Box 900, Hales Corners, Wisconsin 53130-0900. Isn't it beautiful?

Chapter Sixteen

The Seasons of Life

Sadness, Joy, Darkness, Light

In Memoriam

He Loved His Family and The Lord

The Passing of My Husband 2002

My husband, Victor Vanacore, died of cardiac arrest in 2002. His death was not a shock to our family. He'd had open heart surgery 25 years earlier, one year after we moved to California. The children loved their father very much. We buried his ashes under a tree in the mountains west of Las Vegas at Mount Charleston.

My marriage was now completed. I spent a whole year alone. It was a unique experience after so many years of married life. Somehow I felt as free as a bird. I still loved going to the casinos and taking my chances at a poker game. I thought, "What a life! No husband to be accountable to, and no children to take care of! Now it is just *me*." But of course, this did not last, nor did I expect it to. My son Chuck asked if he could move in, since he was in the process of his divorce. There was "no way out" for him but to come back home. As any mother would do, I welcomed him home. I used to say, "I have double doors—and they will always be open." I was only too happy to have Chuck move in with me after his chaotic divorce.

I continued to do my service at the El Jen Convalescent Home, just as I still do to this day. I believe I will continue it as long as I can serve My Lord. I will continue to visit the sick and lonely by bringing our Church and our Jesus into their minds and hearts. This gives me more peace and love than I could ever ask of My Jesus and Mary.

My greatest gift to you is the Holy Eucharist –

His Body given to you …

Go to Church. Jesus is there for you

and for everyone else too!

Gloria Vanacore

A Highlight of My Life 2005

A Rainbow from God

When Victor Jr. was about ten years old, he entered his first music competition, playing the piano, and took second place (a violinist won first place). I realized then what a talent Vic had, and I knew that if he worked hard at his music, he could become a successful musician. So from that time on, we saw to it that he practiced constantly! He did become a *very* successful jazz musician, Hollywood composer, arranger, and conductor, as the following phone call to me one day in 2005 would confirm!

One day in 2005 Vic Jr. who was then living in Granada Hills, north of Los Angeles, called and told me that he had just received a letter from the National Association of Recording Arts and Sciences. They said he had just been nominated for a Grammy Award for his arrangement of

"Somewhere, Over The Rainbow" for the final album made by Ray Charles: *Genius Loves Company!* I said to myself, "Gosh, wouldn't it be *amazing* if he *won* it—proud mother that I am!" Vic would be receiving one of the music profession's highest honors, after devoting so many years of hard work to his music. Music had always been his life! I immediately thought, "Okay. Gloria. Now is *your time to pray!*" I would talk to God and say, "Oh Lord, this is a tough one. Being in the running for this Grammy along with three talented "A-List" arrangers. Is it possible Vic would have a chance?"

The night before the Grammy Awards were to be given out Vic said, "Mom, I don't think we will be able to make Mass tomorrow morning. I'm having a limousine pick us up and there will be too much to do. I hope it's okay with you." I responded, "I'd hate not to go to Mass, since it is going to be a special day." Instead, I suggested, "Let's go tonight. We have time." So we both went to the Saturday night Vigil Mass at Vic's parish and sat in the back of the church. I prayed and asked the Lord to put Vic on His *Eagle's Wings* and fly him to that stage to receive the Grammy, which I felt he so richly deserved. I prayed, "God, please let it be *Your* Will." At that very moment, the church pianist began to play "On Eagle's Wings!" Then the congregation began to sing.

I looked at Vic and said, "You will win the Grammy tomorrow night. I feel it so strongly!" He looked at me and smiled. I really believe he thought I was nuts! He actually *laughed* at me as we got in the car to drive back to his home. I said to him, "Okay, you will see!"

That Sunday afternoon we were all chauffeured in a limousine to the Staples Center in downtown Los Angeles. Of course I was nervous! Who wouldn't be? My son David who is also an accomplished musician said, "Mom, I can take you into the theater so you can go in early and sit down. You can pick your own seat." There were no reservations. It was "open seating." I looked at David and said, "I don't want to sit far back. Your brother is going to win—and we'll be closer to the stage that way." He grinned and must have thought to himself, "There she goes again with her 'pipe dreams.'"

When Vic's category came up, the announcer read the names of all the arrangers who were nominated from a large screen above the stage. Vic Jr. had his head down in his hand. Perhaps he was saying his prayers. I had already talked to My Lord. The list even included David Foster, who was already very well known by then. At the end of the list of nominees, there was a pause that seemed endless while the announcer opened the envelope ... and then ... he said,

"*... and the winner is . . . Victor Vanacore!*"

We shouted and screamed out with joy at the same time! Chills ran up my spine. At that moment, I thought to myself, "Lord! You heard me again!"

How Could I Not Believe!

This story does not end here. Three months later Victor's beautiful wife Noi gave him a surprise celebration party. Somehow she had managed to get a couple of his friends to take him on a trip to Santa Barbara for the day. Back at home his party was being prepared in the garden. His son, Victor Vanacore III, also a great musician, had decided to have live music for the party. He had gathered some of their musician friends together, so that they would be playing when his father arrived home to surprise him. They had also invited family and a few of his "favorite people." I flew in from Las Vegas, and Vic's brother, Paul flew in from Buffalo, New York. Two more surprises!

That day the weather had been overcast and dismal. When my daughter-in-law Lisa (David's wife) picked me up at their home in Valencia, where I was staying, Lisa said, "Mom, start praying that it doesn't rain. Everything for the party is set up outside in Victor's backyard!"

When I arrived we all waited patiently for Victor to come home. Finally our cell phones were ringing! The car came in the driveway along the side of the house and into the backyard. Right on cue Victor's son and the other musicians began to play. Guess what song they chose? Yes!—His Grammy Award-Winning arrangement of "Somewhere Over the Rainbow!" What a touching moment this was for my son Vic and for all of his friends and family! And—as if that were not enough … when Vic got out of the car with the music playing—a beautiful double rainbow appeared in the sky right above us—vibrant and as clear as day! To get his attention I shouted,

"Look, Victor, there are two rainbows in the sky!" Everyone looked up at them, including Vic. That was another great highlight in my life—an answer to a prayer! (The actual photo is at the beginning of this chapter.)

"Children are a Blessing … I will teach your little one music and you will have another musician you will be proud of. Vic and his younger sibling will be working and playing piano together … "

Sister Marjorie

David, my youngest son, is now also composing music for television and movies, giving me a lifestyle I never could have imagined. How could I not believe along with Sister Marjorie that his birth was a blessing from Heaven for me? I am very happy that (his first music teacher) Sister Marjorie's words would come true. She didn't tell me at the time—*and I didn't dream at the time*—that David would be CEO of VANACORE MUSIC, his own music company, and become the composer and arranger of scores for many television series, such as Mark Burnett's "The Apprentice" starring Donald Trump, "Survivor," and many other popular television programs. Someone knew that all of this would happen before it did though and that was my Lord and Saviour.

Children are truly a blessing as Sister Marjorie said. She was so right! I just thought, at the time I was so upset and spoke with her, that I didn't need another child. I thought I was getting too old! How limited my own vision at that moment of what I needed in my life was. How foolish I was, but I am so grateful now!

I have marched against abortion clinics with the Legion of Mary and other Right To Life protest groups. I would like to deliver my own personal message to any mother who does not want to keep her pregnancy or her child – and to those who believe in abortion or do not want to sacrifice to give their children tender loving care: All children are blessings! Our newborn *and unborn* babies are to be loved and gratefully received into this world. They are Heaven's Blessings! Please give them tender, loving care despite hardships and disappointments. They are yours to cherish as the birds take care of their nest, as the shepherds take care of their flock of sheep. "I know My sheep, and My sheep know me," Jesus said. Life can be beautiful—and you with the Lord can make it so.

When David was conceived I thought, "Gosh—do I need another child here? I had my figure back and I loved going back to work. I finally could earn some extra money and buy some clothes for myself, and lo and behold! I thought, "This has happened again? Not again! Lord why me?" Yet little did I know that at the end of my years, David would be My Angel. I say Angel because, even today—not only do I call him that—but people who meet him do likewise. I am also *equally* blessed and proud of my other "Earth Angels": my children, grandchildren, nieces, and nephews. My son Paul is a Components Design Engineer and a part-time musician/entertainer; Madelyn, my precious only daughter, is a highly capable Senior Material Production Control Analyst; Robert who has remained near me and has been a respected and loved professional head waiter for twenty-seven years at the Las Vegas Riviera Hotel is also a talented music teacher; and finally, Arthur (Chuck) who possesses many of his father's skills, is a Certified Marine Engineer and owner of "Chuck's Mobile Marine." All of my children have brought me and those they have touched so many blessings.

Gloria Vanacore (right of photo holding banner) at the Walk For Life March on the corner of Sahara and Las Vegas Boulevard in 1992.

More Angels in My Life

Katelyn Mary Vanacore

My granddaughter Katelyn was born on November 19, 1991. She is the daughter of my son Chuck and his first wife, Cari. The day of her birth was another day on which I never ceased praying. Hers was a Caesarian birth. At the eighth month of pregnancy, she was removed from her mother's womb, operated on, and remained in a paralytic state for one month on a life support system. Katelyn was born with a diaphragmatic hernia, which also necessitated the surgical movement of vital organs. The doctor said at the time of her birth that she was the sickest baby in the world. He told us he had done his best—and said we should keep praying. It looked as if she was going to make it through all of the surgeries. With our diligent prayers we called her our "miracle baby."

When Katelyn was about five years old, I began to take her to my Legion of Mary meetings. She would kneel like an angel and recite the Rosary with all of our members. At that time it was also becoming apparent that she was reading even before she began kindergarten. When I took her shopping with me, she could already read newspaper headlines and magazine covers at the checkout counter. Bystanders would notice this and compliment her. As I cared for my beautiful granddaughter Katelyn, I began to feel contentment in my own life as she and I continued our meetings with the Legion of Mary. Today Katelyn Mary is going to college, is an honors student, and is on the Dean's List. She intends to graduate and work in the medical field— God willing.

"A Miracle in This Earthly Life"

The Life of Zachary John Beveridge

November 25, 1986 - April 24, 2011 Rest in Peace

I stopped writing for some time and, more than ever, I came to realize that I had to complete what I started to write. I began to realize it was the journey of my life, the everyday encounters that occurred, and my love of God along the way that were important for me to share with others. Some things that took place could have been prevented while others seemed almost inevitable. So I have always felt and stressed that all things happen for a reason. There is no such thing as a coincidence. Therefore, the story of our beloved Zach is one I must tell.

Zach was my young great-nephew and son of my niece and godchild, Candy McMahon. He suddenly passed away of a heart aneurism at 3 a.m. on Easter Sunday, April 24, 2011, at his home in Long Island, New York. He was only 24 years old. It was a sudden death—and a great shock to us all. Many phones were ringing on that sad morning.

There were cell phones, e-mails, and Facebook postings. The messages were going miles and miles across the country. Who would ever have realized that young Zach was loved and admired by so many people? What was so special? Why did I choose Zach to write about? There was no doubt as to why I chose to remember him. He was an example of a good, proud young man.

Zach had a beautiful heart which was full of love and compassion for everyone he met. With his sweet smile, people accepted him just as he was. My son Paul described him that way. Paul was a father-figure to Zach who had lost his biological father at the age of two. Zach spent his childhood in Long Island where he was an Altar Server at his parish church. He was also a member of the Catholic Youth Ministry there and involved with religious retreats. He became a team leader so he could share his spirituality with others. At an early age he began to sleep with a cross under his pillow. When his mother was out of town, he would give her a cross to put under her pillow too, so that she could feel connected to him.

Zach touched more lives in his short 24 years on this earth than others touch in a lifetime. His mother, Candy McMahon, told me how dedicated his friends were to him. They loved him so much and believed that he was a man of God. Why, you may ask? It was because of Zach's own deep faith in God. I hope and pray that all his family, friends, and people that knew him have come to believe in and experience the message of faith he left behind. He believed there was a Lord who still loves, strengthens, and gives all of us the courage to go on with our lives according to His Will – and that we should accept all challenges on our own journey home.

Zach later attended Buffalo State University where he graduated in 2008. Because my son Paul lived in Buffalo, he saw him frequently. Zach often visited him and his family. Paul knew Zach better than anyone, and Paul's son Joshua, whose letter to me was in an earlier chapter, was like a brother to him. As for me, I never did get to know my great-nephew that well because we lived so many miles apart. We did have a lot of telephone conversations, short visits, which I still treasure, and time spent together at a few family reunions. All who knew the intensity of Zach's faith in God and his love for his family and friends, especially appreciated the enlightened phrase he had tattooed down the outside of his right calf—*What We Do in Life - Echoes in Eternity*. Thank you, Zach!

The night of the viewing at the funeral home stunned our entire family. Not one of us had any idea as to the large number of people who had been touched by Zach's spirituality and would come to pay their respects. The line of people stretched from the viewing chapel, out past the entrance, down the block, around the corner, and never seemed to end. In his mother's words, "The amazing friend that Zach was to so many people, and the way they looked to him for advice and prayed with him daily, is quite a testament to the way he lived his life. Aunt Gloria was right—Zachary is and always will be my 'miracle in this earthly life.' I look forward to the day that Jesus brings me home to Heaven so that I can be with him in eternity. So now I feel God has something in store for me to carry on." In Zach's honor his mother, Candy, her husband, Mickey, and her sister, Emily started the "Zachary John Beveridge Scholarship Fund." In Candy's words, "We will continue to keep the scholarship alive through Buffalo State College for as long as I live, until the Lord is ready for me."

More Beginning and Endings

As my Life Journey continued, it was soon 2007 and time to sell my home on Coastal Breeze Court. My son David thought the neighborhood was deteriorating, but I was reluctant to sell since I was so familiar with it. I was now living by myself. I was five minutes from El Jen Care Center, ten minutes from my church, and conveniently near stores and my doctor. I think I was just looking for excuses, because I felt so strongly it was the best place for me to be. I have always been a creature of habit, so every now and then, I guess I need a shove. This time I would eventually consider myself *blessed* since the housing market was just beginning to decline. Was the timing by chance or coincidence? By that time in my life, I believed it was the Hand of God that had, again, led me on my way.

This is how it happened: I had met my good friend, Jean Brogan, in a poker room. She was living in the Desert Shores area and knew I was looking for a home. Her neighbor across the street had just decided to sell his house. He had not even put it on the market yet. Jean was so happy and called to tell me I should come over to see it. Immediately I called my son, Robert, who was a real estate agent at the time and lived a few miles away to come over as well. I felt the Lord had to be shining on me, because I loved the house the moment I walked in. I saw a cross and a picture of My Lord on the wall. The ambience of the house felt warm and comfortable, except for the smell of smoke. The home was on the end of a cul-de-sac, so it was private with no traffic.

Robert immediately called David who purchased the house that day. David said, "Mom, if you like it—it is yours!" (After all, didn't Sister Marjorie tell me he was going to be a comfort for me in my later years?) I was so excited! I would finally have a dining room—something I had always desired. The kitchen and living areas all had high ceilings and a look-through rock fireplace between the den and the living room. I could walk into the garage without going outside. The master bedroom was bright and large. It had a bathroom with a closet, shower, bath, and double sink. There was plenty of storage space. In the backyard was a covered patio and a raised flower garden. "How great is this?" I thought, "It's too good to be true after so many years."

Now don't get me wrong. Never in my life did I expect or give a thought to living my life in such luxury! It had always been out of my reach. Truthfully, up until that point I could have cared less, as long as my children were happy and lived comfortably. That had always been my main concern, but as the Lord would have it, he now had other plans for me. Today, living in Desert Shores and having a friend like Jean has been a Godsend. Let's face it—she puts up with my moods! At 90 years of age, my ways of thinking, living, and feeling are all of the "Old School" of thought. Even my children though I know they all love me, as most seniors my age are loved, sometimes think we seniors have a little *too* much to say. Nine times out of ten we tend to openly express our opinions, feeling it is the right thing to do. Too bad we seniors just can't win! The generation of today is not ours.

Which generation is the better one? I will never be the one to make that judgment. The technology and changes that have happened are far beyond what anyone ever expected. Yet one thing that never does and never will change is the *True Word of God!* Most all of my blessings have come in the latter part of my life. Or should I say, I became even more aware of them recently. I was very blessed in my life time and time again!

"All things are possible with God ...
and impossible without Him!" (Mathew 19:26)

My Prison Ministry Ends

I gave up my prison ministry in 2007 after fifteen years, with a feeling of accomplishment. Every Saturday for years I had attended 12:00 pm Mass at St. Joan of Arc's Church. Then I had always walked directly across the street, afterward, to the Clark County Detention Center for my prison ministry assignment. After visiting the El Jen Care Center and the prison every week for many years, I had come to realize that we lay ministers *did* make a difference. Then the Clark County Detention Center added a new wing and there were changes necessitating adjustments for the lay ministry. We had new young people coming in. We had to wait longer to enter the building. I was by that time 83 years old. It didn't bother me that I was older than the rest of the prison ministers. I just didn't have enough patience to wait in the halls for a security guard to accompany me to the assigned rooms. It took time away from my visits with the inmates.

Sometimes we had to do the service alone, because there were not enough ministers. I began to feel it would be better to let the younger laity handle the prison ministry. Then I could just focus on the El Jen Care Center, which was closer—and where I now felt more comfortable. Later I once met several inmates, while ministering at a Halfway House, who recognized me. I was so gratified to learn that they were doing so well—and that they remembered me! I always hoped that our work at the prison would not be in vain. Luthia, Frank, Alice, and Mike—and *all* of you who attended our services—Remember the Lord!

"I know My sheep, and My sheep know me,"
Jesus said. *Life can be beautiful—and you, with the Lord, can make it so!*

... Gloria Vanacore

"Sin City"

I used to thank God that I ended up out here in Las Vegas. At the time I arrived, it was still a "No Man's Land." *Now, they even call it* "Sin City!" *How wrong they all are! Yes, there are a lot of lost souls who need God in their lives here, but, from what I can see, sin is inevitable in the world, no matter where someone lives. How sad I feel when I see this turns of events.*

Serving God here in Las Vegas allows me to share with many others my deep love and devotion to the Blessed Mother and to Our Lord.

Gloria Vanacore

Chapter Seventeen

Peace Found in Las Vegas
A Day in the Life of "Sharky"

I have found a peace here in Las Vegas that I have never found anywhere before. When I moved here, I had already started to ask myself, again and again, who and what was important in my life. I had a real need for fulfillment, but no need to impress anyone. All I really wanted to do, at the time, was to feel good about myself. In a flash I have always realized that I have my children who have always loved and respected me. I have my love for my God who gave me the courage to face the strange encounters I have experienced along the way. I finally began in Las Vegas to realize that I had to give something back to My God, because He had given *me* so much. I believe this is the key to opening up one's heart.

Before my devotion to Mater Dei Chapel and Adoration of the Blessed Sacrament at Elizabeth Ann Seton Parish, I had belonged to the parish of St. Francis de Sales, where I registered first, upon moving to Las Vegas in 1989. I continue to believe that it was really there where I first experienced a real feeling of peace and fulfillment – one that I had never felt before in my life. Yes, I am a mother of six children who are now well-adjusted and bringing up families of their own, of which I am very proud. However I believe that the peace I found working with the Legion of Mary here Las Vegas was something I had searched for all of my life. The Legion meetings began with a review of the two hours of service that we volunteered for weekly, such as visiting the sick, feeding the poor, and praying the Rosary with the elderly at the El Jen Care Center. I was so pleased with myself because of my service to others. I felt as if I was doing good deeds and pleasing my Lord.

I have slowed down now. I'm still playing poker, doing my chores, and visiting my family out of state in California, Utah, and back East. In 2010 I won a seat in the World Series of Poker (WSOP) Tournament, Women's Division. Never in a million years did I ever dream of winning a seat there! Me? Who would ever have thought of such a thing? But the Lord did work miracles in my life. There were 1,000 women playing, and I was eliminated at the "600 Players Level." Now at age 90, I am still playing poker! But today my passion for going into a casino to play has waned; after all, Casinos had been the farthest thing from my mind at age 52 when we moved from back East to California. Today I do enjoy hosting poker games in my home and playing poker at the homes of my beautiful friends. They call me "Sharky"—because no one can read my "poker face!"

A Tuesday Miracle
Hour of Adoration 2008

At some point in 2008 I could neither walk nor kneel. After a series of injections in my left knee, the doctor said that the effects of the series would last for a while, but that nine times out of ten the problem would come back; I would need to have a knee replacement. One morning in 2010 I left the Mater Dei Chapel at St. Elizabeth Ann Seton Church after my hour of Adoration. I felt the pain in my knee again and could barely manage to get in my car to drive home. I called my doctor immediately. She advised me to go to diagnostics and get x-rays, so my good friend and neighbor, Jean Brogan, quickly drove me there. The doctor said it was severe arthritis and, once again, said that a knee replacement might be necessary. I took Motrin for a few days and, of course I prayed.

I never did like to go to a hospital, let alone to start at that time in my life with knee surgery. The following Tuesday morning my visit to the Mater Dei Chapel seemed like an answer to my prayer. There was a strange miracle that day. After my Hour of Adoration, I found myself *kneeling on two knees* as well as walking out of the Chapel! I was able to walk out like a teenager, without pain, and it has been that way ever since! I felt as though the wind was pushing me toward my car, and yet there was *no* wind! I thought this was all rather strange. The following Sunday, I went to kneel in prayer, and again, there was *no* pain—and there has been no pain in my knee ever since. I can even walk on two knees! Was it a coincidence? No!

For some reason the Lord and my Blessed Mother have blessed me with excellent health. Knee surgery? Who needs it? I am enjoying my poker games with a group of beautiful young friends. Forget the knee surgery!

Keeping My Promise

During that time period I also became ill for days with bladder and e-coli infections. I believed then, that these were going to be my final days. I had never experienced this kind of illness. I cried, "No Lord, I can't go now!" All my family and friends knew that I was writing a book. What would they think? That I never kept my word? I was so determined to get well! Before the third or fourth night of my illness, I had a dream—*or it seemed like one!* I saw the silhouette of the Blessed Mary in the alcove of my bedroom. I rubbed my eyes, thinking that I saw two of her, but there was a mirror behind her. Again, was *this* a coincidence? No! After that experience I realized I was going to get well and have another chance at my book. I thought, "Gosh, this is it! I'd better start getting serious before I depart these walls." So I began a new journey again—to finish the book you are reading right now.

Messages and Reflections on Life

About People

I've always loved playing live poker and continue playing today, meeting interesting and beautiful people—and also some not so interesting and beautiful people! It sometimes seems as if, for some people, gambling is their mainstream but it has never been mine. I admit I have enjoyed the *flop*, the *turn*, and the *river*. I still can't believe it myself—winning a seat at the Women's Division of World Series of Poker in 2010 at age 86! What a thrill at my age! Who on earth would ever think it? Little old me! Remember the girls gave me the nickname "Sharky," so you see I'm not the "Holy Roller" some people may think I am. In my heart and in my life, I have met many of the most beautiful people who have all comforted, respected, and loved me.

Why Me ?

Why Not You? God is a mystery and Life is a mystery too. I wonder sometimes why sorrow and disappointment happen to some people but not to others. This is a mystery. A mystery is something that cannot be explained by proof or logic. We don't know all the answers—except to believe in His Divine Will. We are on a journey in Life— believe it or not. And it's NOT all about you! It's about serving God and helping others. The High Road or the Low Road? Take your pick! Left or right? Pick the right way. There is not a middle way There is *only one* road we can choose! If you are wondering what to do, just ask yourself, "What Would God Do?" He is always with you.

My Views on Marriage 2011

In a bad marriage neither partner should endure misery. It is not fair to the children or to themselves. Mistakes are made to be fixed and if there is *no* way to fix them, then there is no other choice but to walk away, hoping a lesson has been learned. Sadly enough, some of us don't learn, and we fall into the same misery madness again. Trust me. I have seen it happen in many families. So what is the solution? I believe we start again. Don't look back. The door that closes opens to a better one. My son Chuck met Nyla, his soul mate, after his first marriage failed. He has never been as happy as he is now. *Thank you, Lord.*

How Do We Ask for a *Favor* from The Lord?

I ask not for myself but for others. I would never ask for money – but instead for guidance. Begin by talking to Him—*one on one*—alone in meditation. Pray with your heart. God knows what you need even before you ask Him.

Here is a quote from Christopher News Notes (No. 300):

Question: I find it so difficult to pray. Where do I begin?
Answer: Just pray as you can. Don't try to pray in a way that is false for you.

How Do We Talk to a Stranger About Faith?

My dear friend and writer just asked me this question. It was not a strange question, because I have been asked this many times before. She began, "Gloria, the other day I was sitting and waiting for my car to be repaired, and a man in the waiting room started to talk to me. He mentioned the subject of belief in a faith and one thing led to another." He said to me, "I want to see some *proof* from a religious faith because I can't believe." I told my friend that I would have said to 'Mr. Unbeliever,' "Oh! How *wrong* you are. Tell me—how did you get here today? Were you able to drive, to see, and to read? Have you ever stopped to think that with the Lord everything is possible and that every step you take is from God? Is it possible that in your lifetime, you never said, 'Thank God?' Or maybe you were not aware that there is an angel on your shoulder that God sent to watch over you. God *is* Love."

On Holidays

When we celebrate holidays, we should remember and worship what actually happened on those days: On *Easter Sunday,* the Resurrection of Christ; on *Christmas,* the Birth of Christ; on *Thanksgiving Day,* thanking God for all He has given us at our Thanksgiving tables! Count your Blessings! This idea seems to have vanished from this earth.

My Message & Love Poem for My Children
On My 85th Birthday

My Message To My Children

"I thank my God every time I remember you."
Philippians 1:3

November 5, 2009:

Dear Children,

You are all that I am and all that I have that has made my life complete. I want to thank each and every one of you for giving me the highlights of my life. I wished the Vanacore Family Reunion would never have ended. But as we all know, all things come to an end—the bad and the good. The good we remember and the bad we try to forget. My mother used to say that all things pass but the good within us stays within us. I thank My Dear Lord and My Blessed Mother for all of you. I am a firm believer in loving, caring, and sharing, and I see it in each and every one of you. Oh! How HAPPY you make me!! Continue to live the Christian Life and the Lord and Our Mother Mary will be with all of you. The Lord says, "Love one another as I have loved you." *I feel this. Thank you for being who you are.*

God Bless You Always and Forever,
Mom

My LOVE POEM To My Children
On My 85th Birthday

LOVE

The Gift of Life

L is to LET GO of anxieties, anger, jealousy and pride. Leave it in the hands of GOD.

O is to OPEN UP your heart and overlook doubts and fears. Where there is an Open heart there is GOD.

V is to VOW TO BELIEVE to believe in yourself. Everything is possible with GOD.

E EACH AND EVERY ONE of you is special to me. Can you **BELIEVE** how special each and everyone is to GOD?

I LOVE YOU
NOW & FOREVER
Mom – Noni
Gloria Vanacore

My Children and I on my 85th Birthday

We all enjoyed our time together as a family at my 85th birthday party in Las Vegas, Nevada. It was so wonderful, celebrating with everyone from all parts of the country from the East Coast to the West Coast. Here I am—the third (and shortest) person on the couch at the top of the photo—surrounded by all of my children. Seated next to me on the left of this photo are my daughter, Madelyn, then my son Chuck. Seated on the bottom, starting from the left side of the photo going toward the right, are my sons Robert and David. Victor Jr. at the far right. Above Victor Jr. and on the far right at the top of the photo, sitting right next to me, is Paul.

Chapter Eighteen

TRUE STORIES
Spiritual Encounters From My Children

There is no life without faith or should I say, "We are not whole." We need a way of life, a love of life. The following 2013 collection of brief stories and encounters of faith in the lives of my family, written in their own words, will prove to you once again that in the words of Fulton Sheen, "The family that prays together stays together."

This is a true story in the blessing-filled life of Victor A. Vanacore Jr. in his own words. He is the eldest son of Gloria Sorrentino Vanacore and Victor Vanacore Sr.:

It was always said that the Angels, who had to stand by, helplessly, because they were obedient to the Father's Will, when their Lord and King suffered cruel punishment and died on the Cross, *bellowed out such an agonizing shout,* it reached to the ends of the earth; the curtain of the temple tore, the earth trembled and the mountains shook.

There were reports of earthquakes and mountains splitting all over the world. One happened in the charming historical coastal town of Gaeta, Italy. Set on a promontory stretching towards the *Gulf of Gaeta*, it is 120 km from Rome and 80 km from Naples. A chapel was built in one of these fissures of the mountain. This mountain, split into two equal parts, is a very impressive sight—bringing pilgrims flocking by the thousands to venerate Our Lord here. "Montagna Spiccata" (Split Mountain) is widely believed to have split at the moment Jesus died on the Cross on Calvary, thousands of miles off in the Holy Land.

I arrived in the town of Gaeta as a "fresh off the plane" teenager of 19 years and was greeted with the sights, sounds and aromas of this seaside fishing community. My only possession was my US Navy issued sea bag and an envelope of orders to report to the USS Little Rock; Flagship of the United Stated Navy Sixth Fleet. There was a Navy band attached to the ship and this would be my duty station. For the next 18 months of my overseas duty, I was a typical teenager who was very motivated and enthralled by what life was offering me. I still am.

I was originally being considered for the US Navy Show Band in Washington D.C. However, because of my capriciousness, I found myself constantly in trouble at the USN School of Music and the commanders at the time did not want this feisty teenager anywhere near WASHINGTON D.C.! Hence, to my chagrin, I found myself assigned to the country where my grandparents originated and where I came face to face with my living God.

I reported to the Chief Petty Officer in charge, and because of my past behavior at the School of Music, he immediately assigned me to clean the band room and I was not granted liberty. Liberty is the permission from the armed forces that allows a serviceman to leave the base or ship and visit the local community. I was denied liberty immediately. I found myself leaning on the ship rail, smelling the local aromas but being unable to experience my Italian culture. I felt disappointed, however not angry. I knew from my parents that I was a handful, and that military service would hopefully change my attitude.

I started playing piano in nightclubs at the age of 13, and somewhere through those years, I missed a few lessons on humility. Talent, whether it is musical, athletic, or academic, is of no use to you as a human being if you do not possess the humility to accompany such a gift. God gives the talent to you, but the humility has to be earned—and learned.

The *Little Rock* left Gaeta for my first sea voyage. I remember how seasick I became and the trouble I got into immediately because I took too much Dramamine and fell asleep on my watch. The officers on the Flag Bridge could hear my snoring and I was standing up! I also suffered from undiagnosed narcolepsy, which did not help.
I was granted liberty at our first port, Barcelona, Spain, for only six hours. I managed to stay out of trouble and made it back to the ship without incident. I had a great time because I took four years of Spanish and was practicing with all the girls.

On our way back to Gaeta, the ship was heading south, down the east side of the Italian peninsula and I could see a huge fissure in the side of the mountain. I asked my friend Arthur Mozeik what it was and he explained to me the story of the Split in the Mountain (Montagna Spicatta). I felt chills as I stared at the mountain and could not take my eyes off of it until we rounded the point and navigated our way to our mooring inside the bay of Gaeta.

Our bandleader granted me another liberty for the afternoon if I would make sure I was back on ship before dark. I was thrilled because I was finally going to eat Italian food and pastry and the wonderful espressos and gelatos. Arthur Mozeik asked me to accompany him to where he and a few band members lived and told me we were going to go hiking. I asked him where, and he grinned at me and said, "The Split Mountain." I was unbelievably excited and could not wait to see how high this mountain was.

As it turns out, Arthur's apartment was in Old Gaeta where there was a military prison, and very close to the split. It was a very quick walk to the mountain and from there we could see the beautiful Mediterranean Sea that sparkled with a blue that I had never seen before. After a while, we decided to walk around the top of the mountain to the beach side. When I saw the beach I went crazy because the sand looked so inviting and the water looked so unbelievable that I got the uncontrollable urge to traverse the mountain toward the beach.

After thirty minutes, we were only about 50 feet above the waves and I decided to dive in and swim to the beach. I had no knowledge of the local water, which I learned later through scuba lessons. I commenced to take my shirt off and dove into the water. It was January and it really wasn't that cold outside. After all, coming from Connecticut, I thought that January in Gaeta was like April or May in the U.S. I was shocked when I hit the water. Not only was it cold, but there was also a rip current against the rocks and no matter how much I swam, I was being pulled out to sea. The beach was getting farther away and so were the rocks from where I dove in.

Eventually, I was pulled out to sea and actually past the promontory, where I could see the split from my position. At that point I knew I was not going to make it to anywhere safely immediately. The waves were breaking over me and the cold water was numbing. I could feel I was swallowing a lot of salt water, but I did not panic. It was at that moment that I remembered the words of my mother. "If you ever need God, all you have to do is call Him and He will be there for you."

I was drowning due to fatigue and I knew it. I had already been pulled down twice and I knew that the next time was going to be my last. They were all afraid because they knew I wasn't going to make it even with help coming. The ship's helicopter would arrive, but only to search and not to rescue. The last time I went under the water, I did not feel cold anymore. My eyes were open and I was praying to God and the Blessed Mother to be with my mother because this was going to devastate her. I always knew how much she loved each and every one of my brothers and our sister. She would always say that she had to die first before any one of us. I remember sinking fast into the sea, but a strange thing happened. It never got dark, as I experienced later as a scuba diver. As a matter of fact, a brilliant white light appeared as I was praying for my Mom and I cannot remember what happened after that. My friends told me later that I disappeared under the water, 200 yards off of the point where the Mountain turns toward the beach.

The next time I experienced consciousness was when I slowly awoke in a kneeling position at the bottom of the Mountain on the seaside with waves pushing me against the very sharp lava rock. As I was gaining back my consciousness I could hear water pouring out of something. When I opened my eyes I realized the water was coming out of me and I was not vomiting. The sound was similar to, as if I was holding a five-gallon bucket and pouring it out. Wow. *How* did I get to the base of this Mountain from out in the sea?

I was eventually rescued by Helicopter after climbing up the mountain to where they could get a Marine down the mountain with some gear. When they pulled me up to the top, the pastor of the Church of the Split in the Mountain was there and he told me what he saw. He said to me that as a priest, he had seen some pretty miraculous things but that this was something special. He took me into the Church. We knelt at the altar and we prayed—Him in Italian and me in English. He asked Arthur what my name was and he addressed me by name. "Vittorio, your life was saved today; the good Lord wants you here for something. You are not ready to go and you will live a long time. Go out and do good things for people. Try to be gentle, kind, considerate. See God in others. Always see the good in people and especially people you do not like. He will answer all of your prayers, but in His time, not yours."

While I found this to be great advice, I also found that it is not easy to do all of these things. I am a work in progress and I pray every day that the Lord stays with me throughout eternity. I have finally learned about humility and I also have realized, looking back, that I was part of God's plan. He was steering my vessel of life and it was He who was in control throughout all of my disappointments. Looking back, in my wildest dreams I never would have guessed what I have accomplished in my life. I made it through a divorce, two wonderful sons, and wonderful wife, and a huge extended family. God has been good to us, and has blessed us all.

Victor Vanacore Jr.,
Granada Hills, California

"I Saw The Light"
Paul Vanacore (2013):

I was born in 1950, Baby Boom Central and from the time I can remember, I'll never forget my life. Growing up, our lives were a very special time that I still reflect on today. My brothers and sister were my best friends and we grew up in a neighborhood right out of the Baby Boom era where everyone had four or more kids and the majority of them were Italian. We were all born in New Haven except for my youngest brother David, who was born in North Haven. We had a childhood like no other. In 1957 my father moved us up to North Haven which was a fairly rural place at that time. There was a small pond that we lived on which became the focal point for a childhood—full of memories of fishing, swimming, and ice skating. If we wanted to play baseball, football or hockey, all we had to do was to call one or two houses and there would be more than enough kids willing to join us (to make teams).

Another special place in my life was 69 1st Place, Brooklyn, New York, where Mom was from. When we visited, it was like visiting Italy but we didn't realize it back then. Everyone spoke Italian, the women cooked, the men ate (and smoked) and the kids—me, my sister and brothers and our cousins, all played together outside on the stoop (steps) of our grandparents' flat, or down the street in Carol Park—where there was everybody from Gloria's Pizzeria (OMG) to Scotto's Funeral Parlor. Movies were made right where we came from! Looking back on it now, it was the "time of our lives!" For me, personally and to this day, my grandparents, Emily and Amedeo Sorrentino, had a profound influence on my life—always loving and nurturing to ALL of their grandchildren, and so special to be with during Thanksgiving and Christmas. It never got old. NEVER GOT OLD!

To this day our entire family of aunts, uncles and cousins (first, second, and now third) remain very close with one another. It is truly a family of faith, love, and togetherness. My father marched off to church with the family every Sunday morning, every Holy Day of Obligation, you name it, and we attended. As we got older, Victor and I became Altar Boys and served Mass for years. After a while we did weddings, funerals and baptisms. We actually made a little money in tips but it was always about our faith. We also had a TV guide route which was like having a paper route but you only had to do it once a week.

As I got older I found myself falling more and more in love with God to the point that I wanted to become a priest, and at 15 or 16 years old, I couldn't be an Altar Boy any more. I was too old. But my love was still there. At the same time this was going on, so were the tumultuous '60s—race riots, demonstrations against our government, pot smoking, hippies, draft dodgers, registering for the draft, burning draft cards and kids fleeing to Canada to escape being drafted. Being born in 1950 put me and my brother Vic right in the middle of this mess.

It was a time of innocence that changed in a moment. If your family could not afford college, you had no choice but to register for the draft and there was a 90% chance you were going to Viet Nam. I remember watching the news at night with my father, leading up to the time of my 18th birthday and my father, who was definitely a man's man, and whose brother Anthony was a WWII hero, was disgusted watching the news.

The next thing I knew, I was in Little Creek Virginia at a Naval Special Forces Training Center getting schooled in

Counter Insurgency (I didn't even know what it meant). It was a Navy "SERE" School meaning: Survive Evaded Resist Escape. It was 12 weeks of heavy calisthenics, hand-to-hand combat fighting, weapons training, five mile run in the AM and PM with full packs, and passing around a 50-caliber machine gun as we ran, obeying the order of "leaving no man behind." If someone dropped, we all had to turn around and pick him up. Nine weeks went by.

Once we were done with this part of the training, we spent three weeks in the swamps of Virginia in July learning to read maps and compasses and trying to make coordinates on the maps. With very little sleep (sleep where you could), no food or precious fresh water, we were harassed all along the way by U.S. Marines and Navy Seals dressed as Viet Cong and North Vietnamese Army soldiers. Once sleep deprivation set in, it was "game on." They looked like the enemy, complete with those slanted eyes. They knew exactly what our coordinates were, attacked us and would beat the hell out of us, pour out our fresh water and disappear as fast as they came in. After two weeks of this, hell started. At the very last check point, we thought the training was over, laughing a little, crying in happiness and then the worst imaginable happened. What seemed like an entire platoon of enemy soldiers had us completely surrounded and force-marched us, for an eternity, to a simulated prisoner of war camp.

To this day, 43 years later, I remember every day we spent being tortured, interrogated, beaten with bamboo sticks (caning), and sleeping outside with nothing on but our skivvies. It seemed like we were awakened every 10 minutes. Again sleep deprivation and brain washing became one in the same. The deal with all of this was for the enemy to try and break down our "Chain of Command" who were the officers and who were the enlisted men. We wouldn't and didn't give them anything. I wanted to go home. I thought I was 25,000 miles away from home and no one would ever see me again. I was in freakin' Virginia and didn't even know it. We were liberated from our POW camp about seven days after we got there. Ironically, the same guys that tortured us, and beat the living life out of us, put on their American uniforms and came to our rescue.

No one will ever know what it was like watching them lower the enemy flag and then raise our flag. We were in formation, the national anthem was being played, and we tried to sing it but there wasn't one guy who didn't break down crying because we were just saved from a certain death. We were in freakin' Virginia but mentally and physically, we weren't. From there, I got to go home for a few days before being deployed to Viet Nam. Oh yeah, another thing, I kept thinking to myself that ALL Navy personnel have to go through this training even if they're going to be stationed on a ship in the Gulf of Tonkin. When I got home and my mother saw the condition I was in, cut, scratched, and bruised from head to toe, I had to explain to her and my father where I was and what I had just gone through. Being so long ago, I can't remember their initial reaction but I know it wasn't good.

The ride to the airport was fairly quiet. No one was saying a whole lot, but then my father turned and looked at me and said something so profound, that I'll never forget his words. "Do you want to go to Canada?" How ironic. I told him I would be o.k. and that the training I just experienced would take care of me. Off we went and my life was never the same. I left behind the most peaceful setting of home, family, friends, and my first love. Never in my wildest dreams could I have imagined the transition and transformation that was about to take place in my life. I completely lost my innocence and the spirituality that I was raised on, that was a huge part of my life.

When I arrived in Saigon (Capital City of South Viet Nam) in 1970, I was told the city was built for 500,000 and was currently occupied by almost 4 million people—mainly refugees but none the less it made Saigon a very dangerous city. The entire country was dangerous, no front lines, and no distinguishing your enemy from civilians. We had no idea who was who. I realized at this point that there was no way I was going to be stationed on a Navy Vessel, but instead I was part of NSA (Naval Support Activity), Saigon, which pretty much explained right then and there WHY I had the training that I had.

No one should have to experience War. War is ultimate suffering. Doing what I did, seeing what I saw, was not fit for a NORMAL man. I'm not sure after years of conflict how the Vietnamese felt, but I know the profound impact it had on me for the rest of my life. It took me three months to be completely torn down—stripped bare of everything I ever thought was good in life, including my spirituality and being born again as a no-good "bad ass."

I questioned my love for my God over and over again—"Please Lord, stop this suffering, please Lord, why must it be this way? Please Lord, help me feed these people—Please Lord, I need to go home where I belong," and so on and so on. I wanted to see my mother really badly for those first three months thinking it was going to happen but it never did. I'll say it over and over again! The suffering those people experienced was next to none— and what for? The average Vietnamese civilian back then earned $100 PER YEAR. I became so angry and no longer cared anymore about anything, family included. While preparing for patrol one day, I was passed a joint (marihuana). I told the dude to get that f'n shit out of my face and then he said to me, "Hey man, if you get blown away, this is the only way to go." I asked if it really made you feel that good, and he replied, "You bet!"

It turned out to be good advice. I never went anywhere without it. I bring this up because I was nothing like this, growing up. I found myself giving other guys the same advice. I had no idea of what I had become. I didn't see it in myself and again I lost all of my values. I had so much aggression in me. I had so much hatred—more toward my government than our enemy (*whoever they were?*). This is how I felt. I stopped writing home, because there was nothing good to write about … "Dear Mom, Things are great here, weather's fantastic, got shot at again, miss you all." What the hell was I *supposed* to say? I can't remember if I was called out for not writing home or that Mom was very nervous that I hadn't written. So the next time in Saigon, I was going over to the USO club to make a free call home. When I got there, half of the building was gone —blown away the day before by a suicide bomber! However, the part where the phones were, was still standing and operational. I called my beautiful mother, who I'm sure was praying for me every day. Actually she had asked, at home, for a sign from God that I was okay, and a couple of minutes later her phone rang! It was me.

Fourteen months in that godforsaken place was enough for me. I counted the days, starting at five months left. I just wanted out! I missed everyone so much.

The one and only highlight of my stay was getting a letter from my father. Why? I'm not sure. It was during the Christmas Season—everyone was gathered around our table and my entire family wrote to me but I never thought my father would write something down, so I was rather taken aback by it. The day I flew out of Tan Son Nhut was one of the scariest days there. The runway ended right where a huge rice paddy field was and the plane seemed to hang out over that field [so much] that it was even moving. Looking out the window I could see Vietnamese working the fields and said to myself, "Please don't shoot us down—not now, not after all of this." What seemed like forever was only seconds but surreal, none the less. I just wanted to go home to Mom and my family and the way of life I knew.

When I returned, I didn't know what I had become. My

family didn't understand what I had become, and except for the first few days at home and being back with [my girlfriend] Susan, I started to get extremely depressed. Everyone, including me, thought I'd adjust right back into the man I used to be, but that wasn't the case at all. If I remember correctly, Mom asked me one morning, "Paulie, what's wrong?" I told her I wanted to be back in Vietnam with my buddies (my own band of brothers). That's when the realization set in, that my home life would never be the same. I wanted to be a hippie, now. I wanted to protest against the war; I hated my government for what they did. I still do! I wanted to fight anyone who wanted to fight. I grew my hair, grew a beard and gave a shit about nothing—not even Susan, and we had been planning on getting married.

I cursed when it was absolutely forbidden in my house. I argued with my father, which we could never do before. One time I argued so badly, I wanted him to hit me, so I could hit him back. No way to live! He called me an embarrassment because of what I became and how I looked. That hurt! THE DEVIL HAD MY SOUL and my beautiful Lord stood in the distance, as if to say, "You have to go down *this* road now my son. Eventually I will be there to pick you up." This was around 1973/4 and it wasn't until 20 years later that I found my place back with my God. He took me full circle, along with something that my brother Victor told me.

I said to Vic, "If He is God the Almighty, why must people suffer, die of starvation, fight and maim each other?

Why can't He stop this? Victor said to me, "Paul, don't you understand that we are just passing through here and that our life doesn't really start until *after* death. God has a plan for us—but not here." Finally everything became clearer to me. I began going back to church and saying my prayers every day.

I know that my soul is His. I know exactly where I stand with the Lord. Now, I realize I had to go through that period in my life to appreciate (even more) how precious life is and "How great Thou art." My children, my grandchildren and my precious Family (including ALL of my cousins and their kids) are the greatest gifts in my life—and my wife Cheryl is my best friend. My children made me realize the Ultimate Sacrifice that God made, giving up His Son for the betterment of others. I saw the Light. He came to me in a dream during my darkest time and now I am at peace with spirituality. He is my life, my love, my reason for living—my everything. But I still hate my government for what they did to us.

Paul Vanacore, Lancaster, New York

To this day our entire family of aunts, uncles and cousins ... remain very close with one another. It is truly a family of faith, love, and togetherness.

... Paul

My Spiritual Encounter
Robert Vanacore (2013):

My mom asked me to write about an encounter in my life. I thought, "She doesn't know what she is asking of me." Maybe she does not know that I do *not* like to write. Gosh, I don't even like to read! When I went to Junior High School, she was called to the school office because I had a pornographic magazine between my school books. It is easy to write that, in my life, I knew I was always protected by an inner gut feeling. Does this make sense to you? Going to church every Sunday with my brothers and sister was a habit, and saying the Rosary was another scenario. I have to admit that I *felt* like I was in the middle after my older sister, Madelyn. I must have said to myself, "This has to stop!" I thought that I would make them pay attention to me, no matter what crazy stunt I had to pull on them. Such as: putting chewing gum in their shoes, getting a water pistol and spraying them when they least expected it, or dumping their socks into the toilet bowl.

So I ended up being the jokester or the odd-ball of our family. Yes, I did have a serious side. I wanted to play the saxophone. I loved the sound of music. But I knew in my heart that my mom and dad did not have enough money for me because my older brothers Vic and Paul were already taking lessons. So I decided to learn on my own, and I did. I spent one year at the Berklee College of Music in Boston. I guess I was not serious enough to continue, so I went out and played on my own, though I wish I would have stayed and continued my education. How foolish I was, not to do that.

One morning, I was heading with a friend for rehearsal at the community college, after working till 2:00 a.m., As I got to the freeway entrance, I said to Rich, "Man, Am I tired! Would you mind if I stopped and got a cup of coffee?" Rich replied, "Let's get it at the college, so we're not late." I said, "Their coffee is not the best. Don't worry, I have an angel in my pocket and we won't be late." So I drove one and a half miles out of the way to get a cup.

While driving into the gas station, a man who worked there said, "Get out of your car! It's on fire!" At first I thought he was talking to someone else, so I stopped and parked the car and then a stench of burning wire came up and almost choked us both. The man who said to get out of the car disappeared. At this time the stench was getting worse. So we jumped out of the car. I grabbed all of the saxophones cases and put them on the sidewalk. Then I looked up and saw that I had parked the car two feet from 30 propane tanks and said, "God, Jesus, I think I need your help!" I jumped back into the car to get it out of there but it would not start. I put it in neutral and tried to push it back a few feet but the car hood was really hot now!

Once again I said, "God help me and the people around me." The man who had left earlier had the sense to call the fire department. When they got the call, they were in the intersection where the gas station was, so in a matter of about one minute they arrived. When they saw where the car was parked, *near propane tanks*, some of the firemen started to have all of the people get out of the area. Then they popped the hood then a five-foot flame jumped out and they put it out with a fire retardant. While making his report he said, "Where were you going?" I said, "To the college." He said, "If the car was on the freeway it would have blown up!" "No shit!" I said.

He replied, "Three inches from your gas line—it would have gone right up and, if it would have caught fire *here*—and set the propane tanks off, we would be minus one corner lot.

Thanks God, Thanks Jesus

Robert Vanacore, Las Vegas, Nevada

Three Miracles

Arthur Michael "Chuck" Vanacore (2013)

I have three stories or shall I say miracles that have happened to me to make me realize that God is good and if you believe in Him and have faith in Him, there is nothing you can't do or endure.

A Miracle of God

One of the miracles in my life is my daughter Katelyn, born with a rare illness; no reason for this to happen, but I believe now it was a test of faith. The doctors said she had a fifty-fifty chance to live and that they did all they could for her. I prayed; we all prayed for her to recover and lead a healthy life. When the doctors told me that whatever we were doing, we were to keep it up because Katelyn's recovery was improving. Doctors never bring faith and religion into a conversation with you, but this one did. He told me that it was a "Miracle of God" that she was beating all odds and recovering so fast.

To this day, 22 years later, my little "miracle of life" is doing great—an honors student and as healthy as can be. I have prayed for her every day of my life, since that day at the hospital when that doctor told me that. So believe, my friends, that God is good and He is real. Just reach out and ask for help and believe.

Why Not Me?

My next blessing is a bit on the humorous side. While moving my horses out from Nevada to Utah on a Sunday morning, I discovered that I was out of hay to feed them for that day and night. While traveling, I kept on asking my wife-to-be that there must be somebody or some store where we could buy two bales of hay. Well, we called every one we could think of, to no avail. I started to get a little worried and concerned so I prayed out loud, "Dear God, there must be a way, or someone to get some hay from, today." I must have repeated that prayer over and over in my head and out loud during the whole trip.

Well, when we arrived in town and were heading down Main Street, I said it again out loud, "Oh Lord, please help us find some hay." I was looking down at the time. When I looked up, I could not believe my eyes. There in the middle of the road were two bales of fresh hay. It was a miracle and to top it off, it was right in front of my wife's church. We were in shock! So again, my friends, God is good. Believe in Him and good things will happen. I hope this is good for you, Mom.

When you have a religious upbringing, life is not so much of a challenge. Having faith in the Lord and believing He is real every day, makes life worthwhile. My life has not always been easy. As a child, I enjoyed watching my dad work. I believe he knew I would be the only one who would follow in his footsteps. My first present was a toolbox. I enjoyed boats and tractors. He and I were close. Being closest to my father, he always had me working and doing things for him. He took us all to church every Sunday. When I was young, my faith was never a challenge, but as life went on, I got away from the Church and the Lord, still believing and thanking God for all the good things that happened, and questioning the bad ones.

Blessed Mother—Be with me!

My mother, who is a pillar of strength and faith, always told me, "Don't say 'Why, me?' Say, 'Why *not* me Lord?'" when things were bad or did not work out the way I wanted them to. She has given me my strength and faith to follow. She has been the Lord's Disciple. I believed for my entire life that her words and wisdom were spoken to me from both her *and* the Lord. I am here to tell you and bear my testimony that God does exist and that Jesus is the Son of God.

One time, while driving my mother home from New York to Connecticut, we were in a very bad car accident. Right as we were about to spin out of control, mother put her arm under mine and said, "Blessed Mother be with us now." We were doing 70 mph and the car spun around two to three times, finally hit the curb, rolled over, and came to rest against a sign on the side of the freeway before a downward grade on a hill. It was a miracle that neither one of us were hurt—not even a scratch. More remarkable was that the first person on the scene was a doctor. We were upside down and I was holding both of us up with the shift handle between us. We weren't wearing any seat belts. After seeing the car, even the doctor told us that it was a MIRACLE. I knew right then that it was my mother's words and her faith that saved our lives on that day that the little sports car was totaled. From that day forward, my own faith and belief in the good Lord Jesus Christ has become stronger than ever. God is good.

The Lightning Strike—Will I Ever Be The Same?

This story is one of the most unbelievable things that have happened to me. Without faith in God, and as a true believer, I do not think I would be here today to tell this story. While working in my shop at home in Southern Utah in a rural area at 6,000 feet in elevation, I witnessed a powerful thunder and lightning storm. It rained so hard and fast that I needed to dig some drainage canals to stop the water from running into my basement. While doing this, there was a huge thunder boom and then a lightning bolt hit the ground right behind me. I'm not sure how far, but it was close enough that the hair on the back of my head and neck stood straight up and tingled.

At the moment of impact, I found myself being lifted off of the ground and was held there. At this point it all came and went so fast, that I really wasn't sure what had happened. It was so close that it had stopped the watch that I was wearing on my wrist, and blew out all of my solar power array and inverters. It was huge!

After I had time to calm down, I thought to myself, "Why wasn't I hurt or dead?" Then it came to me. My gracious Father in Heaven had lifted me off of the ground to keep and save me, unharmed. It sounds crazy! But not unless you can give me another explanation, this is *my* story. I am here today to tell it because I am a true believer that our Heavenly Father does exist and I believe in Him with all my heart and soul. So take the time to say a prayer to Him. He's waiting to hear from you.

Chuck Vanacore, Cedar City, Utah

I am a true believer that our Heavenly Father does exist and I believe in Him with all my heart and soul. So take the time to say a prayer to Him. He's waiting to hear from you.

Chuck

"Thanks, Mom, for all the Faith."
David Vanacore

It was Labor Day, 2006. We were on a beautiful weekend getaway to our favorite place, Mammoth Lakes, California, where we have a second home. Mammoth is a beautiful place in the California Sierra Mountains very near Yosemite. We have been going to Mammoth for 30 years and as far as I can remember, I always wanted to live here. When I had a family, I wanted to share this place with them. When I was able to afford a getaway, this was definitely going to be Mammoth. Five years earlier in 2001, my dream came true, or so I thought. We had a fantastic weekend, fishing and enjoying our family; my wife Lisa, my son Chris, 14, daughter Jessica, 12, and my youngest daughter Emily, 11, and her best friend Hallie, also 11.

We saw bears, we went trout fishing in crystal clear alpine lakes, and just had a magical weekend with the family. We were ready to leave for Los Angeles on Monday, Labor Day. We packed up our *Lincoln Navigator* and headed south on the 395. The mountains are beautiful and even the ride home is majestic, starting at 8000 feet and heading lower through beautiful vistas and pine trees. The kids were watching a movie and I was driving peacefully through meadows and cattle ranches. The first hour of driving was picturesque and quite relaxing. We started to hit minor traffic but it was still flowing pretty good. Along the 395 the highway turns to one lane in each direction. Passing is permitted but only in designated areas.

Most of the traffic was moving south with us, with the occasional vehicle traveling north. Lots of campers and semi-trucks use this artery regularly, and it was Labor Day with most people returning to Los Angeles. I am a relatively cautious driver, especially with my family in the car, so I regularly check my rear view mirror. Out of the corner of my eye, I saw a raised up SUV with huge tires and a very intimidating presence on the road. I begin noticing him from my rear view mirror making bad pass after bad pass, cutting people off and almost causing head on accidents behind me. His erratic driving continued as he made his way up the traffic line while weaving in and out of oncoming traffic, continually putting everyone in his path at risk. I mentioned to my family that there was a "guy back here" behind us that was driving crazy. They all stopped what they were doing and also began to watch; he was never staying in his lane for more than a car or two to go by, before he would go out into oncoming traffic and pass cars again. We were all amazed! It was as if he was playing chicken with a bigger, more powerful vehicle than everyone else, and he was going to be safe, because they would back down as he would approach them.

We saw this man run at least one other car into the dirt shoulder before he came up on our car. Then, he got behind us and waited just a brief second, went back out and started to pass me. When he passed me, I gave him his space so he could get in front of me safely. He decided not to take it, but instead tried to speed up and get in front of the car that was ahead of me. At that moment I had a bad feeling come over me. I can't really explain it, but I said to my family that he was going to kill somebody. I started to become very anxious as everyone in the car was watching. It all happened at lightning speed, but somehow I saw what was about to unfold! I saw it all in slow motion ...

He did it again ... This time he tried to pass two large campers at once, speeding furiously into oncoming traffic. He had great visibility because, once again, his car was raised up and now we were in the flat part of the desert ... The first camper tried to let him in, but once again, he declined and wanted another 50 feet of pavement (let's not forget it was Labor Day, at around 2 PM and the traffic was thicker now) ... As he tried to overtake the last camper, I could see another car approaching the SUV head-on ... I could see it clear as day ... about 100 yards ahead ... He had to have seen the look on her face ... eighty year old Janet, who was driving to Reno after spending time with her family. Heading right into this vehicle ... head-on ... he forced Janet's vehicle completely off the road into the dirt shoulder next to the lane, while he swerved back into traffic with a jerk.

Had she not veered onto the shoulder, they would have hit head-on, and there would have been many deaths, probably in my family. At this point, I was surveying the desert floor for a flat area to get away, just in case they hit. There were boulders and rock formations scattered about and I was looking for a clear path to get out of harm's way. I saw Janet's car on the shoulder, wheels kicking dust up and she was trying to control her car with all her might. The back wheels kept spinning at intense speed because they were trying to grip something. Once her back wheels caught the pavement, her front wheels were pointing directly at my face. Her car shot at me like a rocket. I remember hearing her engine roar out of control, as she came at me. I remember yelling, "Hold on, she's going to hit us!" I saw a clearing in the desert and hit the gas full force as I pulled the wheel to the right, not knowing if we could get out of her way …

In that moment I thought, "My God, help me." I actually thought we were clear and had a moment of peace until I heard the loudest clash of metal on metal, ever imaginable. She hit us so hard on the rear tire, severing the axle. That sent us careening into the desert rolling over and over and over. Some witnesses say three flips, the others six or seven, side over side, with desert dust flying inside the car windows, blowing out. It was like a storm of dust, almost surreal.

The last thing I remembered was being suspended in air for what seemed like seconds. Apparently we were on the back bumper, front wheels pointed toward the sky, and it seemed like we were guided back down to the desert floor, right side up. I thought for sure there was going to be somebody thrown from the vehicle—lying there in the desert. We looked around. There was lots of blood and screaming, and people trying to get us out of the car because we could smell gas. It was total chaos!

My daughter Emily and her friend, Hallie were in the back and got the worst of the impact. Emily was screaming, "My back, my back!" over and over, and Hallie had open cuts on her face and hands. Emily and Hallie were both covered in blood, most of it from Hallie. Chris and Jessica were horrified but seemed deliriously shaken. Lisa went into "mom mode" and somehow pulled the girls in the back row out a window as I got the others out of the car. As a father and husband, I can't imagine anything worse happening to your family.

Many cars stopped to help and in one was a nurse. *Thank you God!* We waited for the emergency vehicles to arrive and to the amazement of the paramedics there were no fatalities out of my car. Our car was crushed beyond repair. (I have photos) We were all put in stretchers and the woman that hit us, Janet, was in bad shape. They took her and Hallie first because they were the worst, while we waited for multiple ambulances. Hallie and Lisa went with Janet and could hear her moaning all the way to the hospital. It was a small hospital. Once we all got x-rays and Hallie got stitched up, you could hear her screaming for miles. I held her little hand the best I could as she dug her nails into me which piercing my skin. Her parents entrusted me to protect their child and I had multiple emotions. I felt bad that I didn't do better, but I knew it could have been worse.

Janet could hear Hallie screaming, since only a curtain separated us. Between Janet's moans, I heard her asking if we were all o.k. What an angel! I asked the nurse if I could talk to her and she looked worried that I might be upset at Janet. I assured her that was not the case. She agreed, so I went to Janet and held her frail hand. I told her that I saw what happened and that I knew it was not her fault. Then I let her know that we were all going to be o.k. I'll never forget the sigh of relief she let out. Like the weight of the world was lifted from her. She said in a faint voice, "Thank you thank you. I'm so relieved." She was worried about us. I proceeded to tell her that they arrested the gentleman in stopped traffic two miles ahead. (He tried to run but the traffic jam helped some good Samaritans chase him down.)

Unfortunately, Janet didn't make it. She died days later from internal bleeding she suffered from the impact. She heroically saved many lives that day. It could have and should have been so much worse. After she hit me, I was already off the road, so no other cars were involved. She hit me so hard that her car just stopped and she absorbed the impact. God was there that day with us, guaranteed. I saw the impacts, beforehand and knew what I had to do before it happened. I can't explain it, but it was in slow motion for me so I had time to react. God also had His Hand in the landing of our vehicle. We could have very easily flipped the other way onto the roof.

Many witnesses were shaken as they expected to see more carnage. The paramedics and medical personnel saw us standing and they were saying, "Where are the people in the accident?" They were all amazed; policemen, firemen, doctors, everyone. The driver who caused the accident was convicted of vehicular manslaughter and spent time in prison. We are not without medical issues. Today, Emily (who also had a premonition of the accident) still has back problems. All of us saw a counselor for a while, and Hallie has needed multiple surgeries for scarring. All in all, we all did okay.

There are things to be thankful for in this life. We were spared that day so we could go on and do important things with our lives—and we have and will continue to do so. I'm sure our children will do so also, and so will Hallie or we would not have survived that day.

Thanks, Mom, for all the faith. I'll always have it and cherish it.

Love you, David

David Vanacore, Santa Clarita, California

Lordinance—My Spiritual Encounter

Madelyn Mary Vanacore Price

Take a few minutes to think about your life, and what it truly means to you. Do you wonder what it's all about? Or do you savor each day as a gift, and know that there is a purpose for it after all?

Your parents lay the foundation for your religious beliefs. You go to church with them on Sundays and, as you get older and are on your own—you may not go anymore. Always too busy, working, or too tired and just don't have time. That was me. Now as I look back, I realize that I was missing the greater Gift of Love and Understanding of The Lord Jesus Christ with whom all things are possible.

I always knew the Lord was with me no matter where I went or what I did. His voice is there inside you. You feel Him with you as you walk through life, and it's a stronger feeling when the times are hard and you don't think you can go any further.

It was a "foggy California morning." I had my little dog in the car and was going to drop him off at the groomer's before I went to work. The roads were wet from the dew and the sun had just begun to come up. I had paid little attention to the tires on my car. I took it in for oil changes when I remembered, and back then your car didn't notify you when it was time for an oil change or your tires were low. Unbeknown to me, the back tires were bald and not just bald, the steel belted material was showing. The front ones were a little bit better, but not enough to grab the wet highway. Because it does not rain that often in California, the road was slick due to wet pavement and oil spots that are only washed off, once in a while, when there is a downpour.

Traveling at about 70 mph in the fog, I approached tail lights which I came upon way too fast. I slammed on the brakes and began to spin. I spun onto an off ramp doing approximately 55 mph. I could not control my car or get it straightened out. My arms and shoulders began to cramp. On my left were guard rails and on my right, an embankment that dropped off around 30 feet. I threw my hands in the air and said, "Lord, help me," shut my eyes and began to cry. My car slowed down some, and actually straightened out from its own weight, and I was on the shoulder of the off-ramp, ripping up shrubs, grass and skidding to a halt. As I caught my breath, I tried to open my door. It was so heavy. I realized my car was hanging off that shoulder, being held up by all the shrubbery and grass that had imbedded itself in the undercarriage.

My poor little dog, jumping all around, jumped into my lap. With all the strength I had, I pushed the door open just far enough for us to get out. I gently closed the door for fear that my car would just roll down the hill. I backed up, took a look and could not believe it was just hanging there. If there had been a passenger in the seat, the weight would have sent us turning over and over, as the car would have plummeted down. A police officer pulled up within a minute afterwards and said, "You are one Lucky Woman!" I replied, "No, I am Blessed."

It took three tow trucks to pull me out. The first truck came and hooked onto the front and tried to pull the car out, but the back wheels began to slide down. The driver was afraid it would pull his truck down with it, so he called for two others to hook into the back and driver's side to pull the car out. I know that the Lord took the wheel and saved my life that morning. There is a grand design for all that happens to us in our lives. As my mom would say, "There is no such thing as a coincidence." My pastor put it this way: "There is no coincidence, there is *Lordinance.*" He is there for you if you ask Him. He may not answer the prayers your way, but He eventually answers them in His way and in "His Time."

A Walk in Heaven

I will tell you my story and let you, the reader, decide was it just letting go of my guilt or did the Lord intervene and take my guilt from me? I live on the East Coast and my mother lives on the West Coast and staying in touch is very important to all my family. After my father passed, she became more involved with volunteering at the hospitals and convalescent homes, saying prayers and giving spiritual guidance. She now attends early Mass a few times a week as well, so she is very hard to get a hold of. We have a standing time for her to call me or vice-versa.

Before my father passed away, my mom was usually at home and easy to reach. On one particular Thursday in February, I called and spoke with my mom for a while and asked about my father, who was still alive at the time. He had gone through cancer surgery a few weeks earlier and was in rehab, scheduled to go home the next day. I had scheduled a visit for my father's birthday and purchased my plane ticket weeks before. His birthday was March 26th. He had decided to have his cancer surgery even though the doctor told him he did not have to have it, his heart would give out before the cancer would take him. But, being the stubborn man that he was, he had to have the cancer removed.

I had told him that I probably should come in February, but he assured me that it was not a "big deal" surgery; he would rather I come for his birthday. I argued with him and my mom but they assured me numerous times that he would be fine. He had come through his surgery fine, except his heart was not beating at his normal rate. So, after a few days in the hospital, he had gone to a rehab facility where he would receive treatment for a few days and then go home. I had called him the second day he was there (on Tuesday), and he said that he was doing well and would be home by the weekend.

It was now Friday at approximately 5:30 PM EST. You know the feeling you get when you need to call someone or should do something as if someone is urging you. I felt like I had to talk to my father. I could not find the number of the rehab facility, so I called my mom. She said, "He is doing fine and they are letting him out tomorrow and not to worry. She gave me the number and I called him at 5:50 PM EST. I called and we spoke about how he was feeling and that he could not wait to get home for his up and coming birthday and our visit. He sounded tired and he told me he was. He was going to take a nap before his dinner. I told him I loved him and could not wait to see him and he said the same. Just before I hung up the phone, I heard him make a gurgling noise. The time was approximately 6:05 PM.

At approximately 6:15 PM, my phone rang and my brother Victor told me he had passed away. “No way,” I told him. “I just hung up with Dad just a few minutes ago.” Victor said, the nurse went into Dad’s room just after our phone call and found the phone receiver on his chest and a Rosary on his belly. He was gone. He had died at the exact time he always said his Daily Rosary—EVERY DAY! I tried to get a flight out that evening but ended up leaving Saturday morning. You have the initial shock, then you grieve—and then, you begin to heal. I could not heal because I always felt guilty about not being there for his surgery, even though my family told me not to feel that way. I carried it that guilt for many years. Every day I would think of my father and say to myself, “I should have been there.” I prayed so long for the Lord to lift my guilt.

Seven years after his death, I had a dream. I had never experienced one quite like this dream, and probably never will again. It was as real as I am sitting down writing about this to you.

My son and I travel to work every day. We work for the same company and have a 15 minute commute. My dream begins on our way home from work. As I was driving, he was napping. I saw a truck coming toward us in our lane. I tried to move out of his way but there was nowhere to go. He was going to hit us head-on. I turned the wheel, so that the truck would hit my side of the car and I prayed that my son would be alright. The next thing I knew, I was in a hospital bed. I could hear my husband sobbing, but everything was blurred. The next thing I knew, I was outside of my body, looking down on myself, lying in bed! It was so vivid! I could see the bruises on my face, and my arms and legs in casts, my husband praying, asking the Lord to take him instead of me. I kept calling out, "What about our son?" But I heard no answer. As I hovered over myself, I was crying, but not real tears.

My mother then came into the room, telling my husband that our son would be fine. She sat down next to him and they began to pray. As I watched in horror, I noticed that my eyelids began to move quickly, almost frantically. All of a sudden, someone grabbed my hand and when I looked up, I could not believe my eyes! It was my dad! He took me by the hand and we began to ascend into the clouds. I asked Dad, "Am I dead?" He just smiled. As we passed all the clouds, I could see beautiful colors—all colors from yellow to lavender, different shades, blues—every color imaginable! There were flowers, everywhere the eye could see. Gorgeous colors, pastels—just what you thought Heaven would be! All this time I was floating up! I would look down and I could see myself lying unconscious with my husband and my mother by my side.

I asked my dad again, "Did I die? And is this Heaven?" He said, ever so softly, "No. You did *not* die, and yes, this *is* Heaven. Walk with me," he said. So we walked. I realized that I could not feel his hand in mine, but I knew he had hold of it. He said, "You do not need to feel guilty anymore about not coming to see me. I am here watching over all of you. I await your arrival when the time comes, so be happy and walk with God. Also, know that there is a place that you will go to before you can come to Heaven. There you will Repent and Reflect on your life. I asked him if it was purgatory but he said a different name, which I don't remember. He also said, "You will be called to Heaven when the Lord knows you are ready to receive Him." Then he pointed out in front of him and said, "We are all waiting for you." And I saw both sets of grandparents and uncles who have passed away. I asked his about a specific aunt and he said, "She is not here yet." It is not that these were sharp images, but more "spirit-like."

I began to cry, and he told me not to, and that it was time to go back. I asked him about my mom and he said that she would be with us here on earth for a long time. As we floated back down, I did begin to cry again. He kissed my cheek, and even though I could not feel it, I knew he had. The next thing I knew, my eyes opened and my mother and husband were hysterically crying. The doctor was there, and said I would make a full recovery. I heard my son's voice, "Mom, are you okay?" He had been wheeled into my room and was fine also. As we all cried, I woke up, crying hysterically. My pillow was wet and tears were rolling down my face. I could hardly breathe. I could not believe what I had dreamed. I called my mother later in the day and she called it a "dream within a dream." I explained to her how real it was and how wonderful it made me feel. I no longer carry the guilt of not going to see my father before he passed, and I was able to have a wonderful conversation with him. I was Blessed and I know it. This dream was the answer to my prayer. I can honestly say to people, if asked, "Do you believe in Heaven?" I can honestly say "Yes. There is a Heaven. I know this and I *believe.*"

Madelyn Mary Vanacore Price,
Martinsburg, West Virginia

How Joshua Found God in Prison
A Story of Interest to All Families:

I can honestly say that God has saved my life. I can't say why for sure, nor do I question His motives. But I am sure that my divine intervention came when I needed it the most. It came when I was in a place so dark and desolate that it was FAR below "rock bottom."

I was a slave. I was helpless, restrained, and so entangled in an addiction that I could see nothing outside of it. Nothing really mattered to me at that point. My family didn't matter, my girlfriend and unborn son didn't matter, and any self-worth I had was non-existent. Anyone in my life was basically a pawn on the front lines of a chess match and the end-game always the same; me getting high.

Of course my life wasn't always in this deteriorated state. Actually, it was just the opposite. God blessed me with a birth into probably one of the best families on the entire planet. It went deeper than just my mother and father, who are two of the most special, caring and un-selfish people I know. I was part of the complete and literal meaning of the word "family": grandparents, aunts, uncles, cousins, brothers, and a sister.

When I look back, it's one of the many things that I thank God for. My life was always so beautiful, so fun, and so full of love that it seems to have materialized from a dream. I've heard it said that "Dreams come true" or that "Blessings do happen." Well that was my childhood and my life. The greatness of it can *only* be attributed to some presence not of this world, but to a Creator of these lives, dreams, and blessings.

It was after my high school graduation that my life started its downward spiral into a place that I could never really imagine. Everything I loved, worked for, and wanted to become, ended up vanishing. As time passed, another "love" crept into my life and started to obscure every other thing that was important to me: I had fallen headfast into an addiction of opiates. The worst part was that I was so completely blind to what was really happening. I could not see myself slipping away. It couldn't have come at a worse time, not that any time is good, but my then girlfriend informed me we were going to have a child. The mixture of emotions hit me like a freight train at full speed. I was scared to death — I was happy but I had a major problem with drug use.

I was never raised to deny my responsibilities, so having the child was the only option for us. Under normal circumstances, I'm sure things would have turned out better, but my life was wrapped up in such a whirlwind that I couldn't tell up from down. I was nineteen years old and

I was seriously not ready to have a child. I was still a kid myself and was on track to prove that I really couldn't even control my own life—let alone be in control of another's. I always knew right from wrong and I knew that I didn't want to be the way I was. It was like the drugs had a mind of their own. They fed off my suffering and my struggles, but I was weak to the point that I honestly didn't care anymore.

Everything fell apart for me. I lost my jobs and was in debt with anyone that I could swindle money from. My relationship with my parents became distant and I always tried to avoid them. These were two people that I loved with all my heart, but I still alienated myself from them because I didn't want them to know the truth. Of course, they knew something wasn't right with me because of all of my lies and financial issues. So, I kept my space, tried to become a stranger, and if I could have felt any emotions at that point, I'm sure it would have broken my heart.

Somewhere deep, deep inside of me, I knew that I hated—truly hated who I had become. I used to try to fight back and not let myself be so weak. I went to a "detox" program and was fine for a couple of weeks, and then went right back at it, worse than before. I cried and prayed to God to help me find myself again because I really felt like I couldn't go on like that anymore. I realized that I was asking God for help, but I was keeping my eyes closed when it came to looking for His answer. Apparently the answer was going to find me before I found it and it completely changed my life forever.

I remember that my father, Paul finally made the ultimatum for me to get help or he would make sure that I'd never see my son. At the time, Giovanni was about two weeks away from being born and I knew that I truly needed help. I went back to the same hospital that I detoxed at and I begged for help, but I was denied. My words fell on deaf ears and I was coldly turned away from professional help when I needed it the most. I was full of despair and confusion, but I still felt that I wanted to get out from under the spell I was in. I owed it to my family and unborn child. I went back home and tried to fight through the excruciating symptoms of withdrawal. One that I heard about the most was the overwhelming anxiety and sleeplessness. It was the worst feeling I've ever experienced in my life so I took a sleeping pill. *Nothing.*

A little while later, I took another one, and so on, until I lost count. I never did sleep, but I came to settle in this waking-dreamlike state. I remember that everything was clouded and hazy. With no fear in my heart, no worry of consequences or repercussions, I calmly walked up to the cashier and ordered her to give me all the money that was in the till. I was in and out in less than a minute with something so precious to an addict, "free money."

I continued on robbing stores because of the sheer simplicity and ease of it. Sometimes I got money and sometimes I didn't. I'm lucky God chose to spare my life because I could have easily been shot and killed or even easier, I could have overdosed. I know that it didn't matter to me. I was at the end of my rope. I was tired of living the way I was and I pretty much welcomed any outcome. I didn't think of my family or girlfriend and child and I honestly had no idea of what I was getting into. Things would never be the same again. I remember that complete chaos followed that day I was taken into custody—both plain clothed detectives and officers alike, stormed my apartment at four in the morning.

I guess this is where God really stepped in to save me and open my eyes. For me, it wasn't one of those things where guys go to prison and convert to religions. It was just something that I truly felt in my heart. Things got much, much worse before I was able to see His blessings, though they were always there. I was thrust head-first into the justice system and for the first time in my life, I truly felt alone and misunderstood. Everything was taken from me; my pride, my humanity and my identity had all ceased to exist. I became a criminal. I became a number, just another face in a jumpsuit whose rights and opinions didn't matter. Nothing from my past life mattered and I was looked at with equal disdain as murderers, rapists, and child molesters. This was a level playing field and I was now in the game. A piece of my parents died that day, as well.

On the inside, I sat alone and literally, in a cold, dark, dirty cell. At that moment, I did the only thing I could and prayed to God from the depths of my heart and soul. I had no belief that I could honestly face what was in front of me and yet somehow, I did. God worked through the people in my life and eventually His presence became clear to me.

Everything that didn't matter in those months started to matter again and I felt a huge void inside of myself. I felt so alone and surrounded by so many strange people that I immediately missed my family with all my heart. One outlet that God had continued to work through in my life had been my parents. I've heard it said that love is one of the true emotions that we get from our Heavenly Father and with all the love that I was surrounded by, there was no denying God's presence in my life. Though my parents were just as broken as I was, they gained their strength from love and God. They knew they had to help me through this, and in all reality, I was still their "baby." At the age of twenty, my life existed in a concrete jungle where "survival of the fittest" became a reality and way of life.

Two weeks later, the best thing to ever happen in my life occurred while I was in the worst place I'd ever been in my life. My son Giovanni was born and I was a father. God blessed me with the most amazing gift that I could ever receive in life. It was the first time I ever cried tears of joy and I was surrounded by strangers who assured me, ironically, that there was nothing wrong with that. I've never been more incredibly intoxicated with happiness and completely condemned to misery at the same time, before. I truly believe that God works in mysterious ways and that everything happens for a reason. For my family, that meant Giovanni. He's the most special child and his presence in life has meant so much without him even knowing it.

After a year of being in the county jail, my sentencing date finally came. My parents were seated in the courtroom and I spotted them easily enough, giving them a weak smile. I had this great speech I had rehearsed a million times and I couldn't remember one word. My voice quivered with such fear that I could barely talk as I stood under the unyielding scowl of the judge. Her face was a stone mask. Her heart was an ice box, and it was clear to see that nothing I said mattered to her. She held my life in her hands and had no mercy as she passed her judgment. It all went in slow motion. The judge gave ten years to be served in the state penitentiary. I heard my parents yell out in disbelief and I was ushered out of the courtroom. I was numb, completely numb to the point where I could feel nothing.

I almost think God eased my pain at that point because I felt a sense of serenity. Another phase of my journey was about to begin. State prisons are the craziest, most unorthodox living environments I've ever seen in my life. At twenty-two years old, most kids are going to colleges, having relationships, and just living life. I was surrounded by drugs, violence, corruption, and had to become a different person. I watched all the violence with a quiet demeanor and I learned how to move. It became routine to always look over your shoulder, to never get lazy, and to never really trust anyone. I became a minority in a population and that automatically meant weakness. The weight pit became my home and I channeled my addiction of drugs into an addiction of working out. I gained fifty pounds. I learned to box to defend myself, because I refused to be looked at as weak.

I prayed to God every night for strength and every day I received it. Even though I lived in a place so full of misery, I was so thankful. I was thankful for my family because most others had none. I was thankful that I would one day be free again because most others had to serve life sentences. I was thankful I was even alive because God opened my eyes and showed me that life is a gift to be loved and cherished, not to be taken for granted.

Over the years, my family has become my world and my reasons for making it through each day. I've never felt closer to all of them and I realized that "family" is the basis of life. As I've grown mentally and spiritually, I've come to have a whole new outlook on life and base it on family and faith. In all reality I'm lucky to be alive and I believe God spared me for a greater purpose. He has shown me that, though I am in a place so dark and desolate, my life is full of His Light and Blessings. I give thanks to Him every single night for every single breath I breathe, for every single family member I have, and for every single experience that has made me stronger.

God will never turn his back on us or give us something we cannot handle. He will see us through our darkest hours and shine His light on us. The night is always the darkest just before the dawn. Every single day is a new gift, a new opportunity, and a new start for us as people to grow and share our love of life. For me, my life will begin again soon. I'll be reunited with all those that I love and adore above all else. I've waited so long, dreamed so much, and never wanted anything more with my entire being. My heart and soul yearns to continue on this path that God has placed me on. With a second chance at life and an opportunity to make things right, I set out to complete destiny with my family and my faith.

From Joshua Vanacore,
Grandson of Gloria Vanacore

Believe And Trust

In The

Word Of God

Chapter Nineteen

Life is a God-Given Gift

On November 5, 2014, I turned 90. Never did I believe I'd still be here. I must admit that most all of my friends and relatives who came before me have gone to rest. But here *I am*—into my 91st year! Just over two years ago, in the summer, I went to swim with the dolphins in Cabo San Luca with my youngest son, David, and his beautiful family. What a treat that they took me there! I am *so* fortunate and do believe in my heart and soul in My Lord.

Where did the years go? I'm still trying to figure it out. So much has happened, and yet—little did I realize why? I always had so many questions. I would ask myself, "Who needs this? I didn't want or expect this. It's not my life. Who ever thought I would end up here?" Haven't you asked yourself questions like that? Of course being a Mom and loving your children is a normal reaction, especially in this day and age. It's strange, though, that we don't often stop to think of what is taking place in our lives. A

"Journey of Life" is what it is. When did it happen? How did it happen? What year did it happen? And most important, *Why* did it happen? It is all there in my lifetime of 90 years.

Whether our children are biological or adopted, we are all children of God—His Creation. As of today I have 15 grandchildren and nine great-grandchildren. Although two of my grandchildren are not biological, I love them as if they were my own. It is amazing how Chuck's son, Richard (biological son of his first wife Cari), has adopted so many traits similar to him. Chuck taught him his trade. Richard now lives in Las Vegas and works in the construction industry. Victor Jr.'s younger son Joe (adopted by Vic after his marriage to Noi) has demonstrated talent and great intelligence in his early teen years and is now in college studying computer science. He is a very caring person like his mother Noi, Victor Jr.'s wife. Noi has been especially helpful to me during my many visits to them in Granada Hills. Noi and Joe were both born in Thailand, and we are looking forward to their becoming American citizens. They've brought much happiness into our family.

How Could I Not Believe?

Now that I am growing towards my last stage of life, I realize that every incident in my life has been significant. For each there was a reason, meaning, or message—at the time, which I could not understand. It all seems so much more clear to me now. The message is always there. Life is a God-given gift, and we must live it to the fullest—loving, believing and trusting in the Divine Will of the Lord. As we go on believing, only then can we see clearly why we are on this special journey—a journey for every soul that the Lord has created. I believe that my experiences with all my children, as well as Joshua and Zachary, mark the most memorable "encounters" on my journey Home.

Living in Vegas became a whole new experience for me. I came here to reside, after I gave up my home in California where I lived for eight years. I am taking my steps here with Him. I realize that for every step I have taken in my entire life, My Lord sent me His Angel who sat on my shoulder. I never believed that I would still today be walking into a convalescent home and having people tell me, "You made my day," or ask me, "When are you coming back?" My experiences in life have also proven to me what an important part the Blessed Mother has played in my life. I never mentioned it to anyone, because it might have sounded like I was "off my rocker" (like my cousin Connie) or simply "off the wall."

For a time I used to get annoyed with myself, as the years went by, because I felt I was not accomplishing anything worthwhile in my life. But now that I look back, I know in my heart that I did. I also know that you too can feel the same way. If you have children, always let it be known how much you love them. They need tender loving care, as well as guidance and discipline. We take *so much* for granted. Many of us are not fully aware of the true meaning of life—what really matters and what doesn't, what is important and what isn't. I realize now that it isn't what you have, but what you *do* with what you have in your life. Our lives are precious gems, given to us by the Almighty. Your children are His gift. Live your life with true meaning to serve Him. Be conscious and aware of God's giving moments and never despair. Life can be beautiful. There is a message God wants to convey to all of us here: mothers and fathers, brothers and sisters, other relatives and friends,

Love One Another!

The End

To order this book or to contact Gloria
please visit:
www.howcouldinotbelieve.com

ABOUT THE AUTHOR

THREE WISHES

I had three wishes and favors to ask of My Lord before 2014 ended. I thank Him today—for they *all* came true!

Wish One

Wish One was Katelyn Mary's college graduation. I never dreamed I would live to see that day. On May 1, 2014 before flying to Florida to attend, I had gone to the chapel for my weekly visit and Novena. I hesitated to go since I was so busy that day. I had so much to do and yet, in the back of my mind, I thought I'd feel guilty not doing my service for My Lord. Oh heck, I thought—three more hours. I will make the best of it. Lo and behold—I drove to the convalescent home and, sure enough, a car came out of nowhere from a parking space. It hit me on my back fender, then hit my car door passenger side. I felt like a truck had hit me! The car kept going, and my first instinct was to follow it. Thank you, Lord, I did! Insurance covered the $3,500 damage and I was spared any injury. I did not need that accident that day. Only the Lord knows why I had to be traumatized that way. It was my last mishap of the year. *Oh, God, how good You are to me!*

Wish Two

Wish Two was that my grandson Joshua, whose inspiring letter from prison and spiritual testimonials you read in Chapters 15 and 18 would return home to our family. Joshua did come home, safe and sound, and attended both our family reunion *and* my 90th birthday party! I was blessed to see my beautiful Joshua there and have my second wish fulfilled by God!

Wish Three

Wish Three was that my book would be published by the end of 2014. Thanks You God, my book **How Could I Not Believe** will be reaching my readers in God's world before the end of this year! You may be reading it right now. May God Bless You!

How Could I Not Believe?

AT MY 90th BIRTHDAY PARTY

On my 90th birthday, November 1x, 2014, we spent the afternoon and evening enjoying a beautiful dinner and party celebrated at the Sun Coast Hotel and Resort! I was thrilled. At the party that evening, I was asked a few questions by the videographer,

"Gloria, how do you feel about your party?"

I answered, "Truthfully, I am overwhelmed! To my amazement, it is much more than I had ever imagined my 90th birthday party would be."

Then I was asked, "How did you do it, Gloria—bringing up six wonderful children?"

I said, "All it takes is to love and to care—to know them and sacrifice for them. With the Lord, it comes easily!!!"

I'm just a Mom who lived it!

I did it God's Way!

I have included the following pages for your own reflections, devotions and prayers. I would also love to hear from you. I welcome you to visit my website or to email me. May God bless you and those you love.

… Gloria Vanacore

Reflections, Devotions And Prayers.

Your Prayers & Reflections

Your Prayers & Reflections

Your Prayers & Reflections

Your Prayers & Reflections

GREAT SKY PUBLISHING
www.greatskypub.com

r73015

27525197R00134

Made in the USA
Columbia, SC
02 October 2018